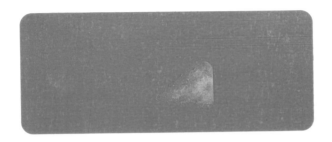

KING RICHARD THE LIONHEARTED

and the Crusades in World History

Katherine M. Doherty
and Craig A. Doherty

Enslow Publishers, Inc.

40 Industrial Road	PO Box 38
Box 398	Aldershot
Berkeley Heights, NJ 07922	Hants GU12 6BP
USA	UK

http://www.enslow.com

J-B
RICHARD

Library of Congress Cataloging-in-Publication Data

Doherty, Katherine M.
    King Richard the Lionhearted and the Crusades in world history /
Katherine M. Doherty and Craig A. Doherty.
        p. cm. — (In world history)
    Includes bibliographical references and index.
    ISBN 0-7660-1459-2
    1. Richard I, king of England, 1157–1199—Juvenile literature.
2. Crusades—Juvenile literature. 3. Great Britain—History—Richard I,
1189–1199—Juvenile literature. 4. Great Britain—Kings and rulers—
Biography—Juvenile literature. 5. Jerusalem—History—Latin Kingdom,
1099–1244—Juvenile literature. [1. Richard I, king of England,
1157–1199. 2. Kings, queens, rulers, etc. 3. Crusades.] I. Doherty, Craig A.
II. Title. III. Series.
DA201 .D64   2002
956'.014--dc21
                                    2001000701

To Our Readers: We have done our best to make sure all Internet addresses in this
book were active and appropriate when we went to press. However, the author
and the publisher have no control over and assume no liability for the material
available on those Internet sites or on other Web sites they may link to. Any
comments or suggestions can be sent by e-mail to comments@enslow.com or to
the address on the back cover.

Illustration Credits: Braun and Schneider, *Historic Costumes in Pictures*
(New York: Dover Publications, Inc., 1975), pp. 45, 75; Enslow Publishers,
Inc., pp. 4, 14, 31, 54, 79, 117; Gustave Doré, *Doré's Illustrations of the
Crusades* (Mineola, N.Y.: Dover Publications, Inc., 1997), pp. 7, 36, 41, 69,
71, 76, 87, 89, 111, 115; Library of Congress, p. 20.

Cover Illustration: © Digital Vision Ltd. (Background Map); Library of
Congress (King Richard Portrait).

Contents

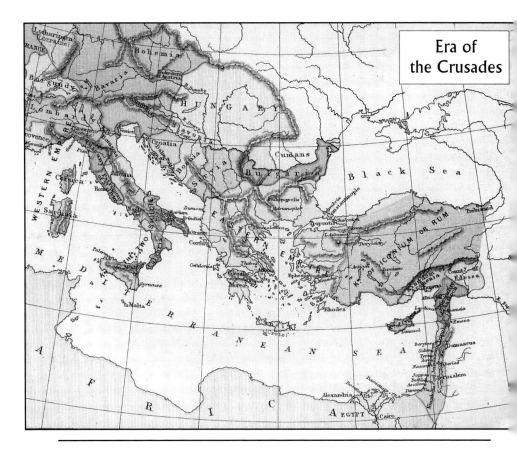

Europe and the Holy Land at the time of the Crusades.

Chapter 1

Rescuing Jaffa

By the summer of 1192, after two and a half years of fighting, Richard I—king of England, ruler of the western quarter of France, and leader of the Third Crusade to the Holy Land—had won many victories against his Muslim enemies. Rather than push on and capture Jerusalem, Richard decided to start negotiations with Saladin, the leader of the Muslim armies, to bring about a satisfactory end to the Crusade.

Richard was conducting negotiations from the city of Acre on the coast of what is today Israel, when word came that Saladin had attacked Jaffa, a fortified port city to the south. Richard was enraged by this attack during negotiations. He quickly boarded a ship with eighty of his knights and four hundred archers and sailed for Jaffa.

As Richard's ship entered the port of Jaffa on August 1, 1192, a priest who had escaped from the city met him and his troops. The priest told them the situation in the city looked grim.

Richard's bravery in battle had earned him the nickname Richard the Lionhearted. This was one of many times that he showed the name was well deserved. As soon as his ship was close enough to shore, Richard grabbed his battle-ax, jumped from the boat, and waded ashore. His eighty knights followed their valiant leader as he led a counterattack on Saladin's army. As Richard rushed into the Muslim army, splitting heads and severing limbs with his mighty battle-ax, many of the attackers were so startled by his sudden appearance that they ran in fear. However, cooler heads soon prevailed on the enemy side, and they realized that Richard had only a small force of knights at his side.

The Muslim forces drew back and reorganized. Then they attacked the city and Richard's small group of knights in full force. Greatly outnumbered and forced to retreat, Richard once again demonstrated why he was considered the first knight of the Christian world. As the Muslims attacked, he and his knights fought an organized retreat that led their enemies into a trap. The four hundred archers who had sailed with Richard had been held in reserve. Now they were waiting to ambush their enemies.

Just as the Muslim fighters came to believe victory was theirs, Richard sprang the trap. His archers fired

As the leader of the Muslims in their holy war, Saladin proved to be a formidable opponent for the crusading armies.

flight after flight of arrows at the tightly packed Muslims. The archers killed or wounded many and forced those still standing to retreat. The Christian forces were once again securely in control of Jaffa.

It would now be up to Richard to get Saladin to agree to an end to the fighting. As the negotiations went on, Saladin showed his respect for his adversary. He told Richard's representatives that he had "long since been aware that your king is a man of honour and very brave . . . he plunges into the midst of danger and in his reckless indifference to his own safety."[1] It was this type of respect from his followers as well as his enemies that made Richard the Lionhearted one of the greatest leaders of the Middle Ages.

Chapter 2

The Middle Ages and the Crusades

The Middle Ages are considered the time in European history from the fall of the Roman Empire in A.D. 476 to the beginning of the Renaissance in the early 1300s. The Roman Empire had existed for over one thousand years, and at its height, it controlled all the lands bordering on the Mediterranean Sea. With Rome as its capital, the empire brought about great advances in literature and the arts and sciences.

When Rome fell in A.D. 476, Europe was thrown into a period of chaos. In many areas, the only law was that meted out by local leaders who controlled only what they could win in battle. Historically, this period continued until the start of the Renaissance, when an interest in literature, art, and science was seemingly reborn.

The Spread of Christianity

During the Middle Ages, there was slow and steady progress toward the conditions that caused the Renaissance to flourish in the fifteenth century. One factor that contributed to the progress of the Middle Ages was the spread of Christianity as it became the primary religion of Europe. The only Christian Church in western Europe at the time was the Roman Catholic Church.

Christianity was based on the teachings of Jesus Christ. Jesus was born in Bethlehem, which is located in the area of present-day Israel. During his life, Jesus wandered and preached throughout the area that is now Israel, Jordan, Syria, Lebanon, and Egypt. The Roman Empire controlled that part of the Middle East where Jesus lived and preached. The Roman rulers of the area thought that Jesus's teachings were dangerous and executed him by crucifixion—nailing his body to a large cross.

Conflicts Over the Holy Land

As Christianity grew, many Europeans wanted to visit the lands where Jesus lived and was crucified. At the same time, the Muslim religion was gaining followers throughout North Africa and in what is today called the Middle East. The Muslim religion is founded on the teachings of the prophet Mohammed, who lived from around A.D. 570 to 632.

As these two religions grew, there was conflict between their followers over areas of the Middle East that were sacred to both religions. Jerusalem is the site where Jesus was crucified. It is also believed to be the place where Mohammed had ascended to heaven. Due to the religious importance of the area, it is often referred to as the Holy Land.

Starting in 1096, a series of wars called the Crusades was fought between Muslims and Christians

Source Document

Urged by necessity, I, Urban, by the permission of God chief bishop and prelate over the whole world, have come into these parts as an ambassador with a divine admonition to you, the servants of God. I hoped to find you as faithful and as zealous in the service of God as I had supposed you to be. But if there is in you any deformity or crookedness contrary to God's law, with divine help I will do my best to remove it. For God has put you as stewards over his family to minister to it. Happy indeed will you be if he finds you faithful in your stewardship. You are called shepherds; see that you do not act as hirelings. But be true shepherds, with your crooks always in your hands. Do not go to sleep, but guard on all sides the flock committed to you.[1]

Pope Urban II started the Crusades when he made this speech at Clermont, France.

for control of the Holy Land. A crusade is a war fought with a religious purpose and at the calling of a religious leader. In this case, it was the pope, the leader of the Roman Catholic Church, who called for the Crusades. There is some disagreement over just how many Crusades were fought. At least eight campaigns between 1096 and 1244 are referred to as Crusades. One of the greatest crusaders was Richard I, who led the Third Crusade from 1190 to 1192.

Chapter 3

Richard the Lionhearted

In 1066, William the Conqueror of Normandy, a part of modern France, invaded England and defeated the English at the Battle of Hastings. In the centuries that followed, one person often ruled both England and parts of western France.

The Rise of Henry II

In 1152, Henry Plantagenet, the duke of Normandy, was eighteen years old when he married Eleanor of Aquitaine. Eleanor was thirty at the time and had been recently divorced from the king of France, Louis VII. Aquitaine consisted of a large part of southwestern France. When Henry's lands were combined with those of Eleanor, he became the ruler of most of western France. As the great-grandson of William the Conqueror and the grandson of King Henry I of

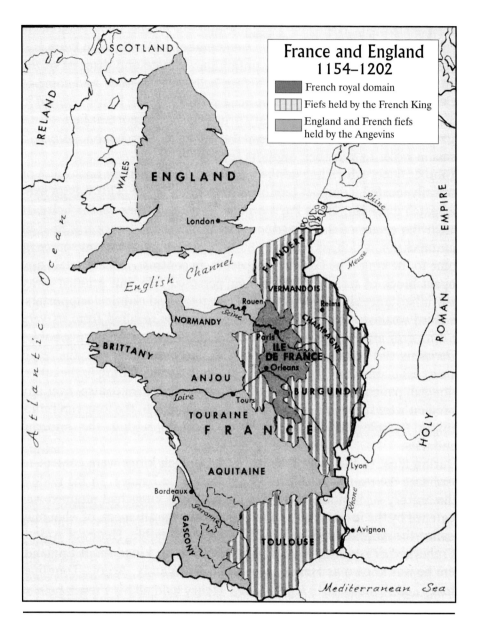

The modern day nations of France and England had drastically different boundaries in the time of Henry II and Richard. The king of England also held land in what is now the country of France.

England, Henry had fought against his mother's cousin, Stephen of Blois, and won the right to succeed him as king of England.

Stephen of Blois died in 1154, shortly after he had recognized Henry as his successor. Upon his death, the twenty-one-year-old Henry Plantagenet became King Henry II of England. Adding England to his own holdings and those he had acquired from his marriage to Eleanor, Henry II became one of the most power-ful men of his time. Despite his power, however, Eleanor spent most of her time in Aquitaine.

Eleanor and Aquitaine

Eleanor was one of the most amazing women of her time. Her court in Aquitaine was the center of a new courtly tradition that put forth the virtues found in leg-ends like *The Song of Roland* about Roland's heroic death in a battle against the Saracens in A.D. 778, dur-ing the time of King Charlemagne of France. Later, these same ideals would be recorded in literature about the mythical King Arthur of England.

It became fashionable for the knights in Aquitaine to expand their learning beyond the military skills of a warrior. They also came up with new rules of behavior for soldiers. The ways of these knights became known as chivalry. Chivalry is a code of conduct that gov-erned the dealings of the armed knights and women at court. A knight who followed the code of chivalry would not use his military skills to take advantage of weaker people. Generally, enemies were treated with respect after they were defeated. Honor became the most prized attribute. The barbaric warfare of earlier times was becoming more organized and began to follow certain honorable rules of engagement. Some of these rules called for prisoners to be treated with respect. Warriors also wanted to defeat their enemies in fair and open combat. Many of these rules continue to govern warfare in modern times. Rules about treating prisoners fairly and with decency and prohibitions against attacking civilians are just two of many examples. The knights of Aquitaine became masters of weapons and fighting, but claimed to use them with honor and fairness. These knights also learned to read and write. They appreciated music and poetry. They subscribed to the ideals of chivalry, although they did not always practice them.

It was in this atmosphere that Eleanor raised her son Richard. Together, Henry and Eleanor had eight children: Henry, born in 1155; Matilda, born in 1156; William, born and died in 1156; Richard, born in 1157; Geoffrey, born in 1158; Eleanor, born in 1161; Joan, born in 1165; and John, born in 1166. As the oldest son, Henry was expected to inherit the bulk of his father's lands and succeed his father as king of England. It was Richard, however, who was his mother's favorite. He spent his early years at her court in Aquitaine. His father named him heir of Aquitaine.

The relationship between Henry and Eleanor was strained from the beginning. Over time, it grew hostile. Unlike Richard, their other sons—Henry, Geoffrey, and John—stayed with their father as he fought against his enemies in France and England. Eleanor saw to it that Richard was brought up in the courtly traditions of Aquitaine. He learned to read, write, and speak several languages. He is known to have written poetry and songs. In addition to being educated, Richard was trained as a warrior. Richard excelled in both aspects of his education. He developed a sense of honor and bravery that others would admire in him throughout his life.[1]

The Rebellious Young Duke

Before his fifteenth birthday, his father granted Richard the title of duke of Aquitaine. Henry II, however, retained actual control over the lands of Aquitaine. He did the same with his sons Henry and Geoffrey in other parts of France. When he was sixteen, in 1173, Richard decided he wanted authority over his own lands. He led a rebellion against his father to win that control. His mother may have been in part behind this attack on her estranged husband. At the time, Henry II was living openly with a mistress and had a number of illegitimate children.

Richard's rebellion failed. He was forced to ask his father for a pardon. Despite the rebellion, Richard had obviously gained his father's respect. Henry II put Richard in charge of subduing those barons of Aquitaine who had been a part of Richard's rebellion. Over the next few years, many of these older and more experienced military leaders were forced to appreciate the abilities of the young duke of Aquitaine. Richard defeated one after another, until Aquitaine was once again firmly united under his and his father's control.

One of the most impressive victories of Richard's early career came in May 1179. At this point, he had subdued much of Aquitaine, but the fortress of Taillebourg was still held by the last of the rebellious barons. It was considered safe from capture. The fortress was built on a high rock outcropping and was surrounded by three walls and three ditches. The small town inside the walls was always well stocked with supplies. It could withstand a long siege, or attack. Rather than attack directly as others had done unsuccessfully in the past, Richard ravaged the surrounding countryside, cutting off all future supplies for the town. Then Richard shocked the defenders of the town by pitching his tents just beyond the range of their weapons and doing nothing.

After a week, the people inside Taillebourg were sure that Richard intended to sit in his tent for as long as it took them to run out of supplies. The defenders decided to send out a force of soldiers to test the strength of Richard's army.

Richard was ready for them when the gate opened. Two days of vicious fighting followed before the town surrendered. To make sure that Taillebourg would not be a problem in the future, Richard had his army level the entire town and all its defenses.[2]

By 1179, at the age of twenty-two, Richard had grown into an imposing figure. At six feet tall, he stood well above the average man of the time. The years of training as a warrior had made his body strong and muscular. His red-gold hair and handsome features made him a royal presence who commanded respect. Despite his royal bearing and military skill, however, it looked as though Richard—a second son—would live his life at the whim of his father and his older brother, Henry.

Sibling Rivalry

None of the four brothers liked the others. As he had done with Richard, Henry II granted his other sons titles to areas of his kingdom but retained control for himself. Their positions as leaders of their separate areas caused conflicts. The fact that the oldest, Henry, would inherit most of Henry II's power also contributed to the bad feeling among the brothers. They were often involved in plots against each other and their father.

One such conflict occurred in 1182. Richard was attending a family Christmas gathering at his father's castle in Normandy. It seems that Henry II was concerned that Richard would not accept his brother Henry's leadership in the future, which would jeopardize all that King Henry II had fought to hold together. Therefore, Henry II demanded that Richard swear allegiance to his brother. Richard refused. The gathering ended in a family feud.

Henry, along with his brother Geoffrey, made a secret alliance with some of the unhappy barons of

Richard the Lionhearted

Aquitaine who had not been able to defeat Richard on their own. While Henry got an army together, Richard rushed home to prepare his defenses. In February 1183, Henry attacked Aquitaine. He intended to teach his brother a lesson. It soon became apparent who would really be the teacher.

As Henry and his forces attacked a fortified church at Gorre, near Limoges in Aquitaine, Richard prepared a surprise attack. The surprise attack was so successful that many in Henry's army were killed on the spot. Many others were taken prisoner. Henry and Geoffrey were lucky to escape because Richard had many of the prisoners tortured and killed. Those who were allowed to live were blinded.

King Philip II of France also stirred up problems between Henry II and his sons. As king of France, Philip felt that Henry II owed him allegiance for his land holdings in France. Henry II did not agree, and often went to war with Philip II over the issue. Any conflict between Henry and his sons could only help Philip gain influence and eventually control in western France.

Richard's older brother Henry was made Archbishop of York. This title gave him a base of power in England to go along with the lands in Anjou and elsewhere in France that his father had already granted him. Richard had Aquitaine in France, and Geoffrey was made heir to Brittany, also in France. This placed the three older sons among the more powerful men in Europe at the time. However, their father still expected their loyalty in all things. When Henry II's youngest and favorite son, John, reached the age of twenty in 1186, Henry II carved him a territory out of the lands he had already granted to John's older brothers. Henry took Poitou and part of Aquitaine from Richard. Anger over this caused fighting between the father and his sons.[3]

Richard Becomes the First Son

In June 1183, when Richard was twenty-six, his brother Henry, heir to King Henry II's throne, died of dysentery at the age of twenty-eight. Dysentery is a disease of the lower intestine caused by a bacteria, parasite, or protozoa. It is often caused by drinking contaminated water. It causes diarrhea, the passage of blood and mucus, pain, and fever. Today, it is easily treated with antibiotics, but in the Middle Ages it was often fatal.

With Henry dead, the players changed, but the problem remained. Shortly after Henry died, Richard's brother Geoffrey was killed in a tournament—a mock battle to help warriors stay ready for battle. Now, as the oldest son, Richard became heir to his dead brothers' lands as well as his father's holdings and titles. Though Richard was now the primary heir, John, the youngest son, remained their father's favorite.

King Philip II of France saw these changes as an opportunity to weaken Henry II's power further. He plotted with both John and Richard separately. England and France were confusingly mixed together at this time. Since 1066, Normans from France had ruled England but were still considered subjects of France. Henry II, as king of England and descendent of the first Norman king of England, William the Conqueror, disputed France's authority over him. His sons, however, lived in and ruled over French territory. Therefore, they owed and gave some allegiance to the French Crown.[4]

Richard Becomes King of England

Over the next few years, Henry II and Philip II were at war over Henry II's lands in France. Richard often allied with the French king against his father. Henry II had ruthlessly used force to rule his subjects and was not a popular leader. Many of his subjects supported Philip II or one of Henry II's sons over him.

In July 1189, fearing military defeat, Henry II stopped the war with Philip II. Shortly thereafter, on July 6, 1189, Henry II died of a fever at the age of fifty-six. Upon his father's death, Richard, age thirty-two, inherited all his father's lands and titles. This made Richard the king of England. He was also in charge of a huge portion of what is today France.

Philip II recognized Richard's claim to Henry II's lands in France. Philip II assumed that Richard was his ally. Richard's holdings in France included Normandy, Brittany, Aquitaine, Anjou, Poitou, and amounted to approximately 25 percent of modern France. According to accounts of the time, many of Henry's subjects were very happy to have a new ruler.

Those who knew him were especially pleased that it was Richard.[5]

Like many rulers of the time, Henry II had forced his will on those he ruled. He depended on his military might to make people support him. Those who went against him were often imprisoned. In contrast to the harshness of his father's reign, Richard began his rule by freeing many of those his father had imprisoned.

Soon after his father's death, Richard left France. He traveled to England, where he was crowned king on September 3, 1189. One of his first acts was to have all those who had been arrested under the Forest Law set free. This law, which had existed for a long time, made it a crime to hunt or gather wood on lands that belonged to the king. Life was hard for many people in the Middle Ages, and the vast lands of the king might be the only source of food and wood during the long winters. This law was so strictly enforced that some people had even been hanged for poaching, or killing animals, on the king's hunting lands. After releasing many from Henry's prisons, Richard went one step further. He pardoned all who had fled their homes to live in the forests as outlaws under the Forest Law. Many of these people were peasants, poor farmers who lived and worked on land that belonged to the nobility, who were just trying to provide for their families. Richard's popularity soared. Unlike his father, he showed that he had compassion and a sense of responsibility toward the common people he ruled.[6]

Chapter 4

Life in the Middle Ages

While Richard lived a life of luxury, growing up in the riches of the court at Aquitaine, life in the twelfth century was extremely difficult for the average person. Constant warfare among the nobility, a lack of knowledge about disease and its treatment, and a total lack of the comforts of the modern world made life short and hard for most people living at the time. Disease and warfare often struck down the leaders of the society at a young age.

Feudalism

Among the peasants, the mortality rates were also very high. The vast majority of people living at this time were part of the feudal system. Feudalism was the main system of ownership and government of the time. Under the feudal system, society was organized by a series of military obligations. The lowest-level member of the ruling class might live in a small, fortified dwelling and control a small area around it. That person would owe allegiance to a lord who might control a number of small holdings and have one large castle in the middle of the area. He, in turn, would owe allegiance and a set military obligation to the next higher lord. This series of obligations would work its way up to the highest-ranking lord, usually the king. As the Middle Ages progressed, kings became more and more important. As this happened, the modern countries of Europe began to form.

At the bottom level of this feudal system were the peasants. They were allowed to live on the land in exchange for their labor, growing crops and keeping livestock. The majority of what they produced was turned over to the lords who controlled the land. The peasants, or serfs, were left barely enough to live on. Any shortage in the harvest could mean disaster for the people at the bottom of the society.[1]

Those at the top of the society lived in comparative luxury, but their lives were ruled by the feudal system as well. The strongest leaders survived and expanded their lands. Warfare among various factions was almost constant. Leaders had to guard against other lords trying to take over their lands.[2]

The most powerful institution of the time was the Roman Catholic Church. The members of the clergy had a unique position. The Church received support from all levels of society. It also owned vast estates of its own. Its power came in part from the international position of the Church and also from its control over the spiritual lives of the people. Many members of the clergy were the younger sons of noble families. They joined the Church because they would not inherit their family lands. In England and to a lesser extent in France, wealth almost always passed from the father to the oldest son. This kept the often hard-won lands of the family intact rather then constantly dividing them up with the next generation.[3] But it also left younger sons with the problem of finding a way to make a living.

Lords, Castles, and Warfare

Many of the landowning nobles, or lords, of the time were only as strong as the castles they built. Richard turned out to be an excellent designer of fortified positions. He was equally good at destroying the castles and fortifications of his enemies. In addition to the strength of the actual castle building, many lords further fortified their castles by surrounding them with high walls and ditches. It became common to fill the ditches with water, which were then called moats.

Capturing a lord's castle often took weeks or even months. These prolonged attacks are called sieges. During a siege, the attackers would surround the fortified position and not allow anyone in or out. The attack was often just a matter of waiting until those inside ran out of food and other supplies.

If the attackers were in a hurry, they could build a variety of siege weapons. One of the most effective was a heavy catapult, called a trebuchet, that could be loaded with red-hot stones. Another effective device was the siege tower. This was a wooden tower with wheels that was built on the spot and could be rolled up close to the castle walls. The siege towers were taller than the walls of the fortress that was under siege. When the tower was moved into position, attacking archers could fire down on the defenders of the castle walls. After the archers had cleared a section of the wall, a drawbridge in the siege tower would be lowered and the attackers could enter their enemy's castle. Attacking armies also used ballistas against a fortified enemy. A ballista was an oversized crossbow that required a small crew to operate it. It fired an iron shaft that was four times the size of a normal arrow.

The Importance of Religion

In studying the history of Richard's time, it is possible to think people spent all their time fighting. Although warfare was a common aspect of life, religion was also extremely important. The Roman Catholic Church was the only official religion for most of what is today called Western Europe. Anyone who did not accept Christianity was called a heathen and labeled an enemy.

There were many older religions in Europe before Christianity. Most of these were based on some form of nature worship. A Mother Nature-like goddess was often the primary figure of these early belief systems. Jews living in Europe at the time were persecuted, and Muslims were the stated enemies of Christianity.

The Church played a major role in the lives of people at all levels of society. The poor depended on the Church for comfort. They hoped that their existence after death would be better than their lives as peasants in the Middle Ages. The Church also provided answers for all the major questions of life. The science and medicine of the time were often nothing more than a mixture of folk remedies and unproven ideas. Despite the fact that members of the nobility maintained their position in society by force of arms, they, too, were dependent on the Church. The Church often served as the middleman in arguments between members of the nobility. If the Church was on a noble's side, he had a strong and powerful ally.[4]

Many people of the time took religion so seriously that they often went on journeys called pilgrimages. During a pilgrimage, the traveler would go to an important religious site in Europe or beyond. Various shrines became important. It was believed that they had the power to heal the sick, or that some other miraculous event had taken place there. To the Christians of Europe, no religious site was more important than the Holy Land in the Middle East. It was extremely important to many Europeans of the time to make a visit to the sites where Jesus Christ lived and had been crucified. They were willing to fight to be allowed to make these pilgrimages.

Chapter 5

Christianity and the Early Crusades

At the time Jesus Christ lived, much of the modern Middle East was part of the Roman Empire, a vast area that included almost all of the lands that border the Mediterranean Sea. In A.D. 476, after repeated attacks by outside forces as well as many internal problems, the Roman Empire came to an end. The eastern half of the Empire, which included much of what is today Greece, Turkey, and the Middle East, became independent. It was referred to as Byzantium. Its capital was Constantinople (present-day Istanbul, Turkey). For many centuries, the Byzantines controlled the Holy Land. Like people in Europe, the Byzantines considered themselves Christians. Their branch of Christianity is often referred to as the Eastern Orthodox Church. However, the people in western Europe recognized the Church of Rome as

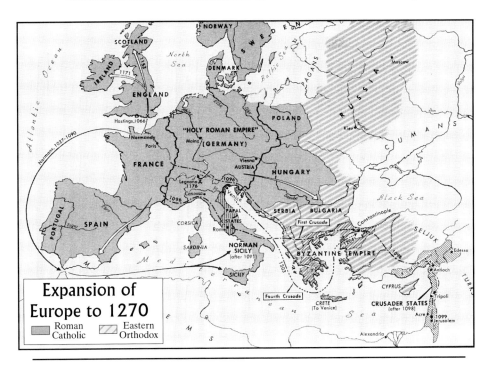

Expansion of Europe to 1270

Roman Catholic | Eastern Orthodox

The split between the Roman Catholic, or western, Church and the Eastern Orthodox Church divided Europe in loyalty to different branches of the Christian religion.

the center of Christianity. The Byzantines had their own Church system centered in Constantinople. Although the two branches of Christianity often disagreed on the practices and beliefs of Christianity, the Byzantines kept the Holy Land open to all Christians who wanted to visit there.

Christians in the Holy Land

The center of the Holy Land was Jerusalem (in modern-day Israel). In 807, King Charlemagne of France founded a hospital and library there for visiting

Christian pilgrims. Because of his generosity, Charlemagne was named Protector of Jerusalem and the Church of the Holy Sepulcher by Haroun el Rashid, the Muslim ruler of Jerusalem. (The Holy Sepulcher was the place Jesus was believed to have been buried.) At the time, Jerusalem was still part of the Byzantine Empire. Hostilities between the Christians and the Muslims of the area were at a minimum. This gave the European Church a link to the Holy Land.

These ties lasted until the eleventh century. At that time, the Byzantine Empire was falling apart, while the Muslim religion was growing rapidly throughout the Middle East. The Muslims took over the Holy Land and many other areas that had been part of the Christian Byzantine Empire. At first, differences between the two branches of the Christian Church prevented any help for the Byzantines from Europe.[1] As the growing forces of Islam gained control of more and more territory, they eventually turned their attention to Jerusalem. A Muslim leader, Caliph Hakim, captured Jerusalem and destroyed the Church of the Holy Sepulcher. This ended access to the Holy Land for Christians.

In 1073, Michael Cerulanius, the leader of the Eastern Orthodox Church, wrote a letter to Pope Gregory VII in Rome, asking for help. The pope quickly raised an army of two thousand men to help regain the Holy Land from the Muslims. However, the army never left Europe. Instead, Gregory ended up fighting a war with Henry IV, the Holy Roman emperor. (The Holy Roman Empire, created in 962, consisted of much of present-day Germany.) Gregory's victory over Henry IV solidified the Roman Catholic Church's political as well as religious influence in Europe. This victory gave him the power to make much-needed reforms of the Church and the clergy. Many felt the Church had become corrupt and had strayed away from its true mission.

The Call for the Crusades

Although Pope Gregory VII never led a Crusade to the Holy Land, the idea of recapturing the birthplace of Christianity appealed to many people. In 1095, Urban II became pope. Thanks to Gregory VII's victories in battle and in reforming the structure of the Church, the Church wielded more power in Europe than ever before.

Meanwhile, the situation for the crumbling Byzantine Empire worsened as it lost more and more territory to the Muslims. Alexius Comnenus, the new Byzantine emperor, sent another appeal to the Western Church for help. The timing of his appeal could not have been better.

For Urban II, a Crusade—a war with a religious objective—to the Holy Land would serve a number of purposes. First in most people's minds was the need to control the Holy Land for religious reasons. But there were many other factors that influenced Urban's desire for a Crusade. By controlling the Holy Land, the Roman Catholic Church would be able to influence the Eastern Orthodox Church. The pope also wanted to end the fighting between the feudal lords of Europe, which was intense. He hoped that sending them together on a Crusade would bring peace in Europe by uniting the nobility of Europe in a common cause.[2]

The Church had declared the Truce of God in 1027. The truce stated there would be no warfare between nobles on Saturdays, Sundays, Mondays, and all church holidays. This left only about sixty days in a year that the Church allowed warfare. Those who broke the truce could be excommunicated, or removed from the Church. At the time, the Church was unable to enforce the truce. It was hoped that a crusade would bring peace in Europe by forcing the nobles to work together.

In November 1095, Urban II addressed a number of church leaders at a meeting called the Council of Clermont in Clermont, France. There, he called for a Crusade to free the Holy Land from Muslims. The Muslims rejected the Christian belief that Jesus Christ was the son of God. Therefore, they were considered the enemies of Christianity.

A number of factors contributed to the positive response the pope received. Europe was in the midst of a population boom that was causing hard times for many peasants. These people saw a crusade as a way to escape their situation. Many younger sons of the nobility also saw a crusade as a way to gain wealth. Others felt moved by religious zeal to go on a Crusade.

At Clermont, Urban II promised many benefits to crusaders. Debts and sins were to be forgiven or postponed. Even more important to many was the pope's guarantee that the crusaders would receive a place in heaven. At the end of Urban II's speech during the Council of Clermont, those listening began to chant *"Dieu li volt!"* which means "God wills it." Over the next nine months, Urban II took his message to other cities throughout France. The excitement for a Crusade spread.[3]

The Paupers' Crusade

To many, it must have seemed as if God's will were at work. Thousands pledged to go on a Crusade. They sewed red crosses on their clothes and painted crosses on their weapons. By the summer of 1096, one hundred thousand people were preparing to join the First Crusade.

Monks, including Peter the Hermit and Walter the Penniless, traveled around Europe preaching the crusade to the peasants. They recruited more than seventy thousand people between them. Their part of the crusade is referred to as the Paupers' Crusade. Between the crusaders of the pope and those recruited by people such as Peter and Walter, some historians estimate that as many as six hundred thousand people left Europe in 1096 on the First Crusade.[4]

The Paupers' Crusade was one of the less noble aspects of the First Crusade. Walter and Peter, because they could not afford to travel by ship, had to

After Pope Urban II first called for a Crusade, several people helped encourage Christians to join the First Crusade. Among these people was Peter the Hermit, seen here preaching to new crusaders.

lead their peasant army three thousand miles overland to Constantinople. Many of those who traveled with them had joined the Crusade in hopes of gaining wealth and adventure. They were not really very interested in the religious importance of the Crusade. This unorganized mass of people had to live off the land as they marched through Europe. They stole crops and livestock as they went. Some went as far as attacking villages, especially Jewish communities, along the way.

In Greece, the crusaders attacked a village they believed belonged to Seljuk Turks. It was actually inhabited by Christians. The people in the town were massacred. At this point, an army made up of Greeks, Hungarians, and Bulgarians attacked the out-of-control crusaders. Many crusaders died in the battle. Others quit the Crusade and went home. Only about half of the original group made it to Constantinople, where they immediately began to cause problems.

Despite suggestions from Emperor Alexius Comnenus in Constantinople that it would be a huge error, many of Peter's followers went on to Nicaea (southeast of modern-day Istanbul, Turkey). Many of the people on the Paupers' Crusade were unarmed. Those who were armed had axes but no armor or protective clothing. Outside Nicaea, the Paupers' Crusade ended in a bloodbath as the crusaders had their one and only real battle with the enemy they had come to fight: the Seljuk Turks. Only about two thousand people returned to Constantinople after the battle at Nicaea. The others were killed or captured. Those captured were sold into slavery and never heard from again.[5]

The Barons' Crusade

The members of the Paupers' Crusade had been on their own. The other armies of crusaders were made up of trained soldiers. They went by boat from Italy to Constantinople and arrived around the first of the year in 1097. This part of the First Crusade is called the Barons' Crusade.

Count Raymond of Toulouse, the most powerful of the barons, was their primary leader. Raymond was a close ally of Pope Urban II. He had already participated in an earlier, smaller campaign against Muslims who had captured part of Spain. Raymond serves as an excellent example of the zeal of the early crusaders. He was among the first to swear allegiance to the Crusade. He borrowed huge sums of money to fund his crusading, pledging his personal property against the loans. Had he not succeeded in the Holy Land, he would have still been duke but would have had nothing left to return to.

Although the main objective of the crusaders was to capture Jerusalem, they fought a number of other battles along the way. The first of these was at Nicaea. Byzantine Emperor Alexius Comnenus had combined forces with the crusaders in hopes of regaining some of the Byzantine territory that had been lost to the Muslims. The combined force of crusaders and

Byzantine soldiers captured Nicaea on June 19, 1097, after a two-month siege.

The next battle for the crusaders was near Dorylaeum, a city in central Turkey. Here they came face to face with a huge army of Seljuk Turks. The large number of Turkish soldiers worried the crusaders at first. They were relieved to learn that the light swords and arrows of the Turkish soldiers did not penetrate their armor.

It was a total victory for the crusaders, and it struck fear in the hearts of those who would later oppose them. Sultan Kilij Arslan, the leader of the Turks' army, always traveled with his royal treasure. After the battle, he was forced to give it up to the crusaders. The sultan's treasure was needed to help pay the growing cost of keeping the crusading army in the field. Everyone involved contributed in some way to the initial cost of raising the army for the crusades. Soldiers were expected to provide their own weapons and horses if they were knights. However, once the Crusade began, the crusaders expected to be able to keep going with the plunder from their victories. By modern standards, their progress was slow. By the time of their victory at Dorylaeum, it was already July 1097.

For the next four months, the crusaders marched through the area of present-day Turkey, restoring Christian rule. They arrived at the fortified city of Antioch on October 20, 1097. Antioch is between present-day Armenia and Syria. It needed to be conquered to protect the land route from Europe to the Holy Land. The city's fortifications were immense. The outer wall of the city was more than six miles long and had as many as four hundred towers. Some of the towers were reported as being six hundred feet tall. The crusaders laid siege to Antioch and were still at it in June 1098.

The crusaders might never have been able to conquer Antioch if one of their leaders, Bohemund, had not bribed a tower guard who was sympathetic to the crusaders' cause. On June 2, 1098, the guard let Bohemund and his soldiers into the city. They opened the main gates, and by the next day, the city was theirs.

The Byzantine residents of Antioch welcomed the crusaders and the defeat of the Turks who had been in control of the city. The crusaders slaughtered the Turkish soldiers who had defended the city for eight months.

Before the crusaders could celebrate their victory, however, the tables were turned. A large Turkish army arrived and laid siege to the crusaders who now controlled Antioch. Rather than settle in for a prolonged siege, the crusaders came out and fought the much larger and fresher Turkish army. Despite the Turks' apparent advantage, the crusaders defeated them on June 28, 1098.

After the defeat of the Turks, the crusaders started arguing among themselves over Antioch. Before the victory, Bohemund had persuaded Raymond and the other leaders to agree to give the rule of Antioch to the leader who was most responsible for its capture.

The crusaders were finally able to win the Battle of Antioch after Christian leader Bohemund bribed a tower guard to allow the crusaders into the city.

He felt his entrance into the city through the guard tower earned him the right to control the city. During the arguments over the future of Antioch, the alliance that had existed between the Europeans and the Byzantines fell apart. The cooperation that had existed from the time the combined Christian army left Constantinople until the victories at Antioch would never exist again.[6]

The Capture of Jerusalem

It was six months before the crusaders finally settled their differences and pushed on toward Jerusalem. In June 1099, the crusaders reached Bethlehem, just north of Jerusalem. Despite continuing disagreements, many of the crusaders were so overwhelmed when they saw Jerusalem for the first time that they wept.

However, it would take more than the tears of the crusaders to capture Jerusalem. The city was in the hands of hostile Muslims. Like most cities in the Middle East at the time, it was heavily fortified. On June 13, 1099, the crusaders attacked Jerusalem and succeeded in storming the outer walls. The inner walls, however, held. Once again, the crusaders' only choice was a siege.

Fortunately, at about this time, ships from Genoa, Italy, arrived with much-needed supplies. With adequate supplies, the crusaders could go ahead with their siege. The nearest supply of wood to build siege towers was fifty miles away. It took over a month to bring the wood to Jerusalem and build the towers. The towers were so massive that it took a thousand people to move them into position.

At this point, there were only fifteen thousand crusaders left. One hundred thousand had left Constantinople a year and a half before this. Because of the time and effort involved in achieving their final goal, the crusaders at Jerusalem became very discouraged. A priest named Peter Desiderius told the soldiers of his vision that they would capture the city in only nine more days if they would walk around the city barefoot, be more humble, and fast for a day. After heeding the priest's advice, the factions within the army set aside their differences and worked together to move the siege towers into place on July 15, 1099.

At first, the crusaders were driven back by the Muslims' flaming arrows. But finally, they got the towers close to the city's inner wall and started firing their own flaming arrows. The siege towers were full of soldiers and had drawbridges that could be lowered to let the soldiers attack the top of the walls. When the first drawbridge was dropped, the Muslim defenders drove the crusaders back and rushed onto the bridge. They did not realize that this was what the crusaders wanted them to do. The crusaders set the bridge on fire and many Muslims fell to their death. Then a second drawbridge was dropped. A small number of crusaders held a section of the wall while a larger force entered the city and fought its way to the main gate. When the crusaders opened the gate, the rest of the Christian army swept into the city, killing everyone in front of them and making the streets literally flow with blood.[7] Almost four years after the call for the Crusade, Jerusalem was in the hands of European Christians.

With this victory over the Muslims, many of the crusaders left Jerusalem. They returned to their homes in Europe. Many others, who had no lands to return to, stayed in the Holy Land and claimed lands there. The barons, who had led the Crusade, chose Godfrey of Bouillon to be king of Jerusalem. He was also called the First Defender of the Holy Sepulcher. A number of other leaders of the Crusade claimed territory in the Holy Land and never returned to Europe.[8]

New Orders of Knights

Many of the nobles joined special orders of knights that were set up in the Holy Land. Two of the most powerful were the Hospitallers and the Knights of the Temple of Solomon, or Templars. The Templars' stated purpose was to guide and protect all pilgrims traveling to the sacred sites of the Holy Land. The Hospitallers were the Order of the Hospital of St. John of Jerusalem. Their purpose was to operate the Hospital of St. John that had been started in Jerusalem. Italian merchants set up the hospital at the end of the First Crusade. After the success of the Crusade, the Hospitallers took on the added responsibility of caring for poor and homeless crusaders who remained in the Holy Land.

The Templars and Hospitallers were part of a new phenomenon. The knights who joined took vows of poverty as well as church vows to work for the good of Christianity and to serve God like a monk. Both

Some knights began new orders after their arrival in the Holy Land. One of these semi-religious groups was the Knights of Templar.

orders became very powerful in the politics of the Holy Land. At one point, the Templars had a series of castles in the Holy Land that were a day's walk apart along the pilgrims' route to Jerusalem. The experiences of the crusaders, both those who returned to Europe and those who stayed in the Holy Land, would have a profound impact on life in Europe.[9]

The Impact of the First Crusade

The period that followed the end of the Roman Empire in A.D. 476 in Europe is called the Middle Ages. It is also referred to as the Dark Ages because many historians believe there was very little advancement in science and technology during this time. The fall of Rome changed Europe, but did not have much impact in the Middle East. In Asia and the Middle East, knowledge of science and technology continued to grow at a faster rate than in Europe. In Europe, however, much of the knowledge gained by the Romans had been lost. The peace and prosperity under the Romans had brought civilization forward. Without Rome in control, much of Europe was left in chaos. Armies of barbarians from northern and eastern Europe destroyed much of what had been the Roman Empire in Europe. It took hundreds of years to recover.

After the First Crusade, trade between Europe and the Middle East created new wealth in the nations of Europe and changed the political landscape forever. The feudal system that was in place was based on land ownership and military control. As trade became more important, the basis of wealth began to shift from land to commerce. The power of kings rose and the importance of unified national governments that could protect trade and commerce began to push out the feudal system. It is these changes that made kings such as Richard I of England and Philip II of France more important than many of their predecessors.

The Europeans traded textiles from England, fabrics from the Low Countries (Belgium, the Netherlands, and Luxembourg), and steel from Germany for luxury goods and exotic foods and spices from the East. Trade existed between the Muslims in the Middle East and other cultures to the East. Large groups of merchants traveled overland with horses and camels to Africa, India, and as far away as China. These groups of traders were called caravans.

The goods Europeans wanted ranged from fine silks to glass for their windows. Some of these trade goods had never been seen before in Europe. Other items had been available but only in very limited quantities and at very high prices. This sudden surge in trade created a need for money. In the feudal economy, goods were often swapped for other items. If someone needed work done by a blacksmith, for instance, and he had some extra cloth, he would exchange goods— the cloth—for services—blacksmithing. The increase in trade and the need to buy goods with money rather than trade for items or services also created a need for banks.

Banking and moneylending were long-established business practices in the Middle East that quickly spread to Europe. In Europe, money began to replace the traditional agricultural barter system. After the First Crusade, powerful European nobles began to pay money to lesser members of the nobility rather than give them grants of land. Some members of the nobility also began to buy and sell land. At the same time, many of the peasants left their traditional homes on the land and moved to towns and cities, where they could work in one of the growing trades for wages.

Peasants in Europe now had a choice of lifestyle. Throughout Europe, new towns began to grow as trade centers. Many of these towns were also involved in making the goods Europe traded with the East. The peasants could stay and work on the land as their families had done for centuries, or they could go to the new towns and cities that were producing trade goods. Many chose to make this move, which gave them a freedom they had never known before. Towns became important centers of population, wealth, and power. As wealth shifted away from the land toward commerce, the traditional nobility began to lose its power base. Nobles had depended on the fact that everyone was tied to the land. As peasants began to leave the land for towns, the nobility lost its laborers and the wealth that peasant labor generated.[10]

Chapter 6

The Second Crusade

Despite the growing trade between Europe and the Middle East, problems seemed to plague the situation in the Holy Land. As soon as the majority of crusaders went back to Europe, problems arose for the Europeans who stayed behind. Bickering among them over who should rule what was one problem. The more serious threat came from the Turks.

It had been Muslim Turks who had originally taken the Holy Land from the Byzantines. When Imad ad-Din Zengi became the leader of the Turks in 1128, he wanted to get back what had been lost in the First Crusade. The crusaders never controlled much of the Middle East. They controlled a thin strip of land from Constantinople to the Holy Land that served as the overland route for pilgrims coming from Europe. This route passed through land controlled by the Muslims.

In addition, the Europeans controlled Jerusalem and a strip of land along the Mediterranean coast. This area is now part of Syria, Lebanon, and Israel.

Muslims soon recaptured a number of towns along the pilgrims' land route to the Holy Land. By 1145, the Europeans who had settled in the Middle East had lost so much territory to the armies of Zengi that many Church and secular leaders called for a Second Crusade. This Crusade was intended to drive the Turks back from the strategic locations along the pilgrims' route.[1]

Fighting the Turks

There were many reasons for the kings of Europe to go on a Crusade. They were in part moved by religious reasons. They wanted to ensure that the Christians of Europe could continue to make pilgrimages to the Holy Land. It was also important to keep trade flowing between Europe and the Middle East.

The Turks who had taken over much of the territory that had been part of the Byzantine Empire were hostile toward Christians. If these Turks controlled the Holy Land, they would likely shut off the supply of trade goods flowing from the East. European control of the Holy Land would make sure that trade could continue.

King Louis VII of France raised an army of twenty thousand soldiers. Conrad, the emperor of Germany, a part of the Holy Roman Empire, also brought along twenty thousand soldiers. The Second Crusade began as these two armies left Europe in 1146 and planned to meet in the Holy Land.

The Second Crusade met with disaster almost immediately. In October 1147, Conrad set out for Nicaea. Half his army traveled overland from Constantinople to Nicaea. The other half went by ship. First, the land group was attacked by Turks near Dorylaeum and suffered huge losses. Then, the group traveling by ship arrived at Nicaea and was also defeated by the Turks who had recaptured the city. Between the two battles, Conrad's force was reduced to between six and seven thousand soldiers.

The rest of the Second Crusade was almost as disastrous. In February 1148, the French crusaders arrived in Attalia, a Byzantine city on the Mediterranean coast. They intended to sail to Antioch. However, there were not enough ships for everyone. King Louis and his knights went by ship and sent their servants and foot soldiers by land without any leadership. Most of those who left for Antioch on foot never got there. Some died of starvation. Turks killed many and captured approximately ten thousand Europeans. Still others, wishing to avoid the Turks, starvation, or death, quit the Crusade and returned to Europe. The problems did not end there.

Once they arrived in Antioch, things continued to go badly. Louis's wife, Eleanor of Aquitaine, who would later become the wife of Henry II of England and mother of Richard I, had accompanied her husband on the Crusade. Eleanor's uncle, Raymond of Antioch, was their host. When Louis was ready to go on to Jerusalem, Eleanor refused to leave. Rumor said she was having an affair with Raymond. King Louis had his wife forcibly removed from Antioch and brought her along with his army. With Eleanor in custody, Louis led his army on to Jerusalem.

Once Louis arrived in Jerusalem, he joined his force with Conrad's. The two leaders drew up plans to continue their campaign to strengthen the European presence in the Holy Land. They agreed to attack Damascus, Syria, which was ruled by the only group of Muslims who were at all friendly to the Christians in the Holy Land. At Damascus, it seemed as if the crusaders would capture the city. Then, for some unexplained reason, the Christian army retreated to an open plain on the outskirts of the city. There, the Muslim defenders of Damascus beat them.

On July 28, 1148, the remnants of the Second Crusade returned to Jerusalem in defeat. Not only was the army defeated, it was disgraced. There were even rumors that Louis and Conrad had accepted bribes from the leaders of Damascus to pull back their forces. The point of the Second Crusade had been to keep the Turks in check. It had also been intended to ensure a safe overland route to the Holy Land for Christian pilgrims. Instead, Louis and Conrad had mismanaged the situation so badly that thousands of lives were unnecessarily lost. When they finally did fight, it was against some of the only friendly Muslims in the Middle East. Because of suspicions about the motives

Source Document

There they found themselves located far from access to water, deprived of the abundance of fruit, and lacking almost all supplies. They were saddened and they discovered, all too late, that they had maliciously been led to move from a region of abundance.

The food supply in the camp began to run out. Before the men had set out on the expedition, they had been persuaded to believe that the city would be quickly taken and they had brought along provisions for only a few days. This was especially true for the pilgrims, nor could they be blamed for it, since they were unfamiliar with the country. . . .

Thus a company of kings and princes such as we have not read of through all the ages had gathered and, for our sins, had been forced to return, covered with shame and disgrace, with their mission unfulfilled. They returned to the kingdom by the same route over which they had come. Henceforth, so long as they remained in the East, they regarded the ways of our princes with suspicion. With good reason they turned down all their wicked plans and henceforth the leaders of the Crusade were lukewarm in the service of the Kingdom. Even after they had returned to their own lands they constantly remembered the injuries they had suffered and detested our princes as wicked men. . . .[2]

During the Second Crusade, the Christian armies suffered a terrible defeat when they tried to attack the Muslims at Damascus, Syria. This account of the event was given by William of Tyre in 1148.

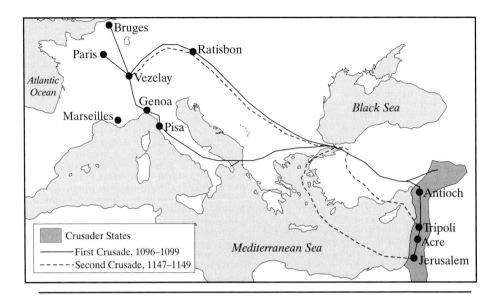

The first two Crusades won control of major regions in the Holy Land, where Christians set up new orders of knighthood and put their own leaders in charge of new governments.

of the leaders of the Second Crusade and their total lack of positive results, the whole idea of crusading in the Holy Land suffered a serious setback.[3]

The Aftermath of the Second Crusade

After the Second Crusade, the situation continued to worsen for the Christians in the Holy Land. Raymond of Antioch was killed in battle in the summer of 1153. The last Christian victory before the Third Crusade began came at Ascalon, the Muslim city closest to Jerusalem, on August 19, 1153. From that point on, the Christians lost the Holy Land piece by piece.

There was also a new enemy in the Holy Land. A Kurdish warrior by the name of Saladin rose to power among the Turkish Muslims. Saladin was from Kurdistan, an area of the Middle East that is now divided among present-day Iraq, Iran, Syria, Turkey, and Armenia. He was born in 1138 near the modern city of Tikrit, Iraq. The area had earlier been converted to the Muslim religion and had fallen under the rule of the Turks.

Saladin rose in power and position by distinguishing himself in battle. He became the commander of the Muslim forces in Syria in 1169. He was called on to assist the Egyptians because the Christians in the Holy Land had tried to expand their lands into Egypt. When he was successful in repelling the Christians, he was named vizier, a position of respect and power in the government of Egypt. When the ruler of Syria, Nur ad-Din, died in 1174, Saladin was chosen by the other leaders in the area to succeed him.

As the leader of Syria and the vizier of Egypt, Saladin's lands surrounded the Christian settlements in the Holy Land. At this point, Saladin and his followers declared a *jihad*, or holy war, against the Europeans living in the Holy Land. Because they were Christians, Saladin and his Muslim followers considered these people enemies. On October 2, 1187, the European forces that had controlled Jerusalem since the end of the First Crusade lost the city to Saladin.[4] It would take another crusade and a bold leader to try to win it back.

Chapter 7

Richard I and the Third Crusade

The fall of Jerusalem was a defeat that rippled throughout the European world. In response, Pope Urban III sent out the call for a Third Crusade. The first nobleman to pledge himself to the Crusade was Richard, one of the sons of King Henry II of England. Henry II was not pleased with his son's seemingly rash decision. However, Richard's life took on a singleness of purpose that it had not had before.[1]

Richard Pledges Himself to the Crusade

Richard's greatest talents were as a warrior and military leader. The Third Crusade gave him a cause that he felt was both just and heroic. The chivalrous traditions he had been taught at his mother's court in Aquitaine were perfect for a crusader. Here was a cause that would allow him to go after the enemies of Christianity with the full support of the Church and the vast majority of the people in Europe. In Richard's mind, the crusade made the wars he had fought with his neighbors in Aquitaine seem petty. He would now be fighting not only for glory in this world but for the glory of heaven in the afterlife.

Despite his enthusiasm, Richard knew that he would have to make careful preparations before he could leave on a crusade. There were two major issues that concerned him. First, he would need to raise large sums of money and outfit an army for the journey. Second, he would need to arrange his affairs at home so that his brothers and father would not try to take over his lands in Aquitaine during his absence.

The solution to the second problem seemed to be the easier one to solve. His neighbor to the south, King Sancho of Navarre (northern part of modern Spain), agreed to protect Richard's lands in Aquitaine. But before Richard could leave, his father began to stir up trouble.

At Henry's urging, some of the nobles in Poitou, a province in the northern region of Richard's lands, rebelled against Richard. As soon as Richard defeated them, Raymond of Toulouse, his neighbor to the east, seized a group of merchants who were on their way to meet with Richard to discuss improving trade in Aquitaine. Henry was behind this as well.

At the time, Richard employed a large force of hired soldiers from the Brabantine region of the

Netherlands. These troops attacked Raymond's lands in the French region of Gascony to get even with him. Raymond's soldiers soundly defeated Richard, who barely escaped. He was forced once again to make peace with his father.

At this point, Henry II of England and Philip II of France went to war. The money Richard and others had raised for the Third Crusade was spent instead fighting the French king.[2]

Richard Becomes King

When Henry II died on July 6, 1189, Richard became king of England. As king, he might easily have been absolved from his pledge to lead the Third Crusade. The responsibilities of ruling his father's vast territories would have been an acceptable excuse to leave the Crusade to someone else or to postpone it indefinitely.

Instead, the opposite occurred. Richard chose to fulfill his pledge to the pope. Succeeding his father as king of England gave Richard the resources to raise the money to wage war in the name of Christianity.

Richard used many ways to raise money in England and his holdings in France. When a new king came to power, all the nobility were expected to pledge their loyalty. This relationship of loyalty to the king is known as fealty. As an act of fealty to their new king, the English nobles were required to get new charters for their positions. (A charter is an official document granting a nobleman his lands and position.) A substantial fee was involved in reissuing these charters.

For the most part, the nobles paid. After the harsh treatment the people had received from Henry II, the people of England were happy to have a new king. This instant popularity aided Richard. If a noble did not pay, however, there was always someone else who could take his place. Under the feudal system, a nobleman held his lands and titles in the name of the king. As king, Richard could take lands away from one noble person and give them to another, as long as he had the military power to enforce his decisions.

The rising importance of the towns of England after the First Crusade also provided Richard with an opportunity to raise money. The wealth of the towns had been a result of the increase in trade with the east. For a fee, Richard granted these growing towns the right to govern their own local affairs. This was one more step toward the end of feudalism and the beginning of modern government. Not only did this provide Richard with the money he needed, but it also gave him new and loyal allies in his power struggles with the nobles.[3]

Richard spent only three months in England after his coronation before he returned to France to complete his plans for the Crusade. England was left in the hands of Richard's twenty-three-year-old younger brother, Prince John. John was to continue to supply the money that Richard would need to succeed in the Holy Land.

With the situation in England settled to his satisfaction, Richard could now direct his full attention to the Crusade. In December 1189, Richard left England with an army of eight thousand soldiers for France, to meet with King Philip II. Richard was successful in convincing Philip to join him, and the two kings swore a pact of allegiance. Richard also agreed to marry King Philip's sister, Princess Alice of France.[4]

Richard and Philip Set Sail

A series of delays kept Richard and Philip in France for ten more months before they finally sailed from Marseilles, France, on the Mediterranean coast to Genoa, Italy, and then on to Sicily. At the time, it was impossible to sail directly from France to the Holy Land. The ships of the day were not large enough to carry all the people, horses, and equipment needed and still have room for enough supplies for such a long voyage. When they reached Sicily, a large island off the southern tip of Italy, it turned out that Richard had other business.

Richard's sister Joan had been married to the king of Sicily. He had recently died. Tancred, the new king, was holding Joan prisoner in order to prevent a conflicting claim to the throne.

Richard's first order of business was to attack Messina, one of the major port cities of Sicily. Richard and his army sacked the town with relative ease and freed his sister. The delays in France, and now the fighting in Sicily, however, upset the timetable for the crusaders. It was now too late in the year to sail eastward. The crusaders had to spend the winter in Sicily.[5]

During the winter of 1190 Richard's mother, Eleanor of Aquitaine, arrived in Sicily to make a change in her son's marriage plans. To seal an alliance with King Sancho of Navarre, Aquitaine's southern neighbor, Eleanor wanted Richard to back out of his engagement to Princess Alice of France and become engaged instead to Princess Berengaria, Sancho's sister. Richard, who often seems to have followed his mother's advice, agreed to make the change. Philip II was not happy. This was the beginning of problems between Philip and Richard that would continue throughout the Crusade.

By the time the arrangements for Richard's marriage to Berengaria were worked out, the Christian period known as Lent had begun. It was against the religious custom of the time for people to get married during Lent. The couple agreed to be married later, when they reached the Holy Land. It was now time to sail eastward.

An Unscheduled Stop to Conquer Cyprus

Three days after leaving Sicily, a storm struck Richard's fleet. The ships were scattered across the Mediterranean Sea. The ship carrying Richard's sister Joan and his fiancée, Berengaria, was forced to take refuge at Cyprus, an island in the eastern Mediterranean. Isaac Comnenus, who had taken the position as emperor of Cyprus, though he had no right to do so, was a Muslim and an ally of Saladin, the

Muslim leader who controlled the Holy Land. Comnenus offered the women shelter. He planned to hold these important women hostage once he had them under his control. Comnenus, however, underestimated his opponent. Richard had no intention of paying any ransom. He proceeded to attack Comnenus's stronghold near the city of Nicosia, Cyprus. Within fifteen days, the emperor was Richard's prisoner. Cyprus was now under Christian control.

Comnenus pleaded with Richard not to put iron shackles on his ankles and wrists. Richard, always a gentleman, honored his prisoner's wishes. He had special chains of silver made to lock up Comnenus. Although Richard had not originally planned to capture Cyprus, he knew that control of the island would help the crusaders throughout this campaign and in the future. Richard knew that Cyprus could be an important stopping point for ships going to and coming from the Holy Land. It was the perfect place from which to supply the crusading armies along the coast in the Holy Land.

Marriage, Then on to the Holy Land

Richard left a garrison and governors in Cyprus to keep things under control for him. With the success of the fighting in Cyprus, Richard decided to take care of one other piece of business. On May 12, 1191, Richard and Berengaria were married. She was crowned queen of England. Berengaria would end up being the only

Source Document

Richard's fleet stopped first at Crete, then at Rhodes, and, on what was supposed to be the last lap of the journey to Palestine, the fleet ran into a storm off the Island of Cyprus. This turned out to be an opportunity for conquest. . . .

When the King learned of the hardships of the shipwrecked men, of the stealing from them, and about the other things which had meanwhile befallen them, he was deeply grieved. The next day, a Monday, he sent two knights as emissaries to the Emperor and peacefully asked him and his men to make voluntary satisfaction for the injuries which had been done and also to restore in full the goods stolen from the shipwrecked men. . . .

The King at once cried out and ordered all his men: "Arm yourselves!" They obeyed immediately. The King armed himself and set off with all his men in the skiffs of the transport ships to land in the port.

The King had with him, at this point, only about fifty knights. He, indeed, was emboldened by their fear. Letting his horse go, he charged swiftly at the enemy. He broke up the enemy's crowded battle line by charging through it. He dealt now with this group, now with that one, and in short order, he dispersed them all. . . .[6]

On his way to the Holy Land, Richard I stopped in Cyprus, where he overthrew the reigning government and set up his own.

queen of England never to set foot in the country. The marriage between Berengaria and Richard seems to have been one of political convenience. The two never really lived together as husband and wife.[7]

After their military successes in Sicily and Cyprus, Richard and his army were ready to face Saladin and his Muslim army in the Holy Land. The battles to come would prove much more difficult than the relatively easy campaigns they had fought so far.

The Third Crusade

The Third Crusade is often referred to as the Kings' Crusade. When it was being planned, three kings agreed to raise armies and join forces: Richard I of England and Philip II of France were to be joined by Frederick Barbarossa, or Frederick I, the Holy Roman emperor.

In May 1189, Frederick I started out before the other two kings. He chose to travel the overland route to the Holy Land. By June 1190, Frederick I had led his army into what is now Turkey. On June 10, 1190, while his army was crossing the Calycadnus River (now the Göksu River) in what was then called Cilicia (part of modern southern Turkey), Frederick I drowned. His army lost its will to fight when its leader died. Many of the soldiers headed back to Europe. Of those who went on with the Crusade, many were either killed or captured by the Turks. Most of those who were captured were sold as slaves.[1] Those who joined Richard founded a group called the Teutonic Knights.

The Siege of Acre

Guy of Lusignan, the reigning Christian king of Jerusalem, had been besieging the Turkish-held city of Acre (located on the northern coast of Israel and now called Akko) for almost two years. Before Turkish leader Saladin's capture of Acre in 1188, it had been a Christian city since its capture during the First Crusade eighty-eight years earlier. Guy was relieved to have additional help from his European allies. Three years earlier, Saladin had defeated Guy. In exchange for his freedom, Guy had promised not to fight against Saladin. It was a promise that he had broken almost immediately. Although most of the noblemen involved in the Crusades followed the new practices of chivalry, these rules seemed to apply only when dealing with other Christians.

French King Philip II arrived at Acre on April 20, 1191, with ten thousand soldiers to assist Guy. With these additional troops and supplies, Philip and Guy were able to build a number of siege engines and increase the pressure on the Muslim defenders of the fortress of Acre. Using catapults they built, they pelted the walls and buildings inside the city's fortress with huge rocks.

As many as one hundred thousand Christian knights and soldiers may have taken part in the siege of Acre. This total included the armies of Guy, Philip II, Frederick I, Richard I, and various other groups that were already in the Holy Land, including the Hospitallers and Templars. There was also a number of smaller independent forces that had come from Europe. It is estimated that more than half of the Christian army died. Famine and disease killed many more Christians than did Saladin's army.

The Christians were forced to stay in their camp on the outskirts of Acre for over two years. They depended on supplies arriving by sea from Europe. The vast tent city they erected lacked proper sanitation. The crusaders were hot in the summer and cold and damp in the winter. During rainy times, the entire camp became a sea of mud. At times, food was scarce. Conditions were perfect for spreading diseases such as dysentery, cholera, malaria, yellow fever, and others that passed through camp. Despite all this, the crusaders attacking Acre remained positive. New recruits arrived from every corner of Europe almost daily.

The arrival of Richard and his army on June 7, 1191, gave the attackers another boost in morale. Because of his military victories in his homeland, Richard was considered the first knight of Christianity by many of the crusaders. Most were eager to follow him as he took over command of the combined forces. One crusader who was not happy to see Richard take command, however, was Philip II of France. Philip was very jealous of Richard's popularity.

As elated as the Christian soldiers were to see Richard arrive with his army, the Muslim defenders of Acre were discouraged. A couple of days before his arrival, Richard had sunk a Muslim supply ship headed for Acre. The supplies on that ship would not reach the people inside the city. Richard also set ships in position to block the harbor of Acre. Those inside the city had no chance of getting any additional supplies.

During the final days of the siege, Richard became sick with malaria, a disease carried by mosquitoes, which causes fever and fatigue. Richard did not let this slow him down. When he was feeling well enough, he could even be found working on the siege engines alongside his soldiers.

By July, the situation inside the walls of Acre had become desperate. On July 12, 1191, the city surrendered to the combined armies of Guy, Richard, and Philip.[2]

By this point, the relationship between Philip and Richard had become quite strained. It had been a serious blow to their relationship when Richard decided to marry Berengaria instead of Philip's sister, Alice. The final days of the siege at Acre further strained the relationship as Richard took command of the combined forces. Richard was a better soldier and the soldiers were more willing to follow his lead. Each crusader, to a certain extent regardless of his home country, was independent when it came to fighting. He could follow whomever he felt would lead the troops to the greatest success. Philip, although an excellent

The crusaders under Richard I were very successful partly because of their use of very strong siege weapons, like this massive catapult, which could rapidly destroy Muslim defenses.

politician, was not a great soldier. When the city of Acre surrendered, Philip decided he had had enough of crusading. He quit the Crusade and headed home to France.[3]

Richard Takes Charge

Philip's departure left Richard as the only remaining king on the Third Crusade. Richard's first order of business was to arrange a prisoner exchange. Saladin agreed to free fifteen hundred Christians, pay two hundred thousand gold dinars (a common currency of the time), and return the holy relic known as the True Cross in exchange for the release of the twenty-seven hundred Muslims who had been captured at Acre. (The True Cross was believed to be a part of the cross on which the Romans had crucified Jesus Christ almost twelve hundred years earlier.)

Richard was not satisfied with Saladin's offer. He demanded that a number of high-ranking Christian noblemen also be released. Saladin, however, did not want to return these well-trained fighting men to his enemy. He refused to change his original offer. When negotiations broke down and Saladin refused to make the payments he had originally offered, Richard felt he had to show the Muslims that he could be even more ruthless than they were. He also did not want to have to waste his resources feeding and guarding twenty-seven hundred prisoners.

On August 20, 1191, Richard had the Muslim prisoners marched to the plains outside the city, where they could be seen by Saladin's Muslim army. Once they were in full view, Richard's army slaughtered all twenty-seven hundred prisoners. Many historians have been critical of Richard's violent actions after the capture of Acre. But Richard knew he could not easily use his

In one of the most controversial incidents in the history of the Crusades, Richard massacred his Muslim captives after the Battle of Acre.

resources to take care of the captives, so in the context of the time and place, it was thought to be a justifiable act. The Muslims were not known to treat Christian captives with great kindness, either. Those crusaders the Muslims did not kill in battle were often sold as slaves. Despite its cruelty, it was said that the slaughter of the Muslim prisoners at Acre gained Richard the respect of his new adversary, Saladin.[4]

Source Document

The Christians, on reaching the middle of the plain that stretches between the hill and that of Keisân, close to which place the Sultan's advanced guard had drawn back, ordered all the Mussulman prisoners, whose martrydom God had decreed for this day, to be brought before him. They numbered more than three thousand and were all bound with ropes. The Christians then flung themselves upon them all at once and massacred them with sword and lance in cold blood. . . . On the morrow morning our people gathered at the spot and found the Mussulmans stretched out upon the ground as martyrs for the faith. They even recognized some of the dead, and the sight was a great affliction to them. The enemy had only spared the prisoners of note and such as were strong enough to work.[5]

A Muslim observer described the massacre of the prisoners at Acre.

Richard's ruthlessness extended to his dealings with the people on his own side, as well. One of the leaders of the Christian army was Duke Leopold of Austria, who had been at Acre for much of the siege. When victory finally came, Leopold hoisted his flag next to those of the kings of England and France. He hoped to claim an equal share of any spoils from the victory. Richard, however, had no intention of recognizing the duke as an equal in this or any other battle. Some of Richard's English knights immediately tore down Leopold's flag. Richard refused to punish the knights or have the flag restored to its position. After such a grave insult, Leopold had two choices. He could challenge Richard's authority and possibly end up fighting him, or he could leave. Like Philip II, Leopold decided to go back to Europe.[6]

The Next Battle

The main objective of the Third Crusade was to free Jerusalem from Saladin's control. To do that, Richard knew it was important to have a solid position on the coast of the Holy Land. So, rather than march directly toward Jerusalem, he had his army head south along the coast. Staying along the coast served a number of purposes. It allowed Richard to stay in contact with his ships, which could easily resupply his army. It also meant that there was at least one direction from which no enemy could attack.

Two days after the slaughter of the prisoners at Acre, Richard and his army marched south. The army stayed in close formation, expecting attack from the Muslims at any time. Small groups of Muslim cavalry harassed the Christian army as it marched along. The effects of these small attacks were minimal because Richard kept his knights in the center, surrounded by tightly grouped foot soldiers. The soldiers wore thick quilted linen coats that the Muslim warriors' arrows could not penetrate. In addition to being protected against arrows, the foot soldiers carried long lances. These weapons prevented their attackers from getting close enough to use their razor-sharp curved swords, known as scimitars.

Richard's plan was to go down the coast and capture Jaffa, a major trade port for the region, now part of Tel Aviv, Israel. On September 7, 1191, on a plain near Arsuf, before the Christian army reached Jaffa, Saladin mounted a full-force attack against Richard's rearguard. The rearguard was made up of Hospitallers. Twice, the Grand Master (leader of the Hospitallers) asked Richard for permission to charge the attacking Muslim army. There were ten thousand Turks as well as a number of Saracens and Bedouins (non-Turkish Muslims allied with Saladin) attacking the Christian army. Richard tried to hold his forces back for as long as possible. However, just as Richard was about to give the order to attack, one of the Hospitallers, Baldwin Carew, an Englishman, charged on his own. The other knights of his order joined him.

Following Carew's lead, the entire army threw itself at the Muslim forces. Saladin had never faced

Other crusading knights created the Order of St. John of Jerusalem, better known as the Hospitallers. In later years, even women joined the ranks of the Hospitallers.

such a charge of European knights before. He learned a costly lesson. His light calvary was no match for the heavily armed and armored Christians and their huge horses. The Muslims' arrows and swords bounced off the European armor, doing little or no harm. Many of the Muslim soldiers fled from the battle on their own.

Realizing the error of his ways, Saladin called for the remainder of his army to retreat. Thousands of Muslim warriors were killed in the initial charge of the Christians. After this battle, Saladin gained even more respect for Richard. This would be the last time during the Third Crusade that Saladin would openly attack the Christian army.

This battle pointed out the major difference between the fighting philosophy of the Europeans and

Richard and Saladin's armies fought valiantly at the Battle of Arsuf. Despite being outnumbered, however, Richard's troops were able to triumph over the Muslim forces with their inferior weapons.

the Muslims. Saladin's army was made up of excellent horsemen on fast and maneuverable horses. The modern Arabian horse is descended from the cavalry horses of the Muslim holy wars. To take advantage of their horses' speed and mobility, the Muslim cavalry had to be relatively lightly clad and armed. Their bows were short and could not generate enough force to penetrate the European armor. Their scimitars were also relatively light in weight, as was the small amount of armor they wore.

For the European knights, the opposite was true. They rode huge, sturdy warhorses that are the ancestors of today's heavy workhorses. Not only could the warhorses carry a knight and all his armor and weapons, but the horses themselves wore their own armor and were trained to be weapons in their own right. Many of the beautiful moves that a horse does in the modern sport of dressage come from the fighting moves used to aid a mounted knight during a battle.

The difference between the Christian and Muslim fighting methods would be like modern warfare if one side had tanks and the other side had jeeps. The jeeps would be faster and more maneuverable, but when they came face to face, the tanks would crush the jeeps every time. This is basically what happened every time Saladin's army openly fought Richard and his knights.

Jaffa and Ascalon

After the Christian victory near Arsuf, the Muslim troops stationed along the coast abandoned their forts rather than face the wrath of Richard and his army. Richard's treatment of the Muslim prisoners at Acre might have frightened many in Saladin's army. As Richard continued south to Jaffa, he twice turned his army inland toward Jerusalem. However, both times he turned back because of concerns that he could not maintain his supply lines. Saladin had destroyed all the crops and orchards that had been established by the Christians who had settled in the area, to prevent Richard's army from living off the land.

Eventually, Richard stuck with his plan to secure the coast first. Rather than try to defend Jaffa, Saladin destroyed as much of the city's fortifications as he could and then abandoned it. When Richard and his troops arrived, they immediately began rebuilding the city.

An event took place at this time that could have changed the history of the Crusades. In addition to being a great warrior, Richard was also an excellent falconer. Falconry is the sport of hunting using trained birds of prey. Richard had brought some of his hunting birds to the Holy Land. September 29 is the Feast of St. Michael the Archangel, a Catholic holiday honoring St. Michael, whom the Bible names as one of the leaders of heaven in the fight against hell. On this feast day, Richard took some time off from his efforts to rebuild Jaffa to go hunting with some of his companions. As they followed their hawks and falcons across the countryside, they forgot, for a moment, about their enemies. A large patrol from Saladin's army happened on the king and his hunting companions and attacked them. Richard barely escaped with his life while four of his companions died ensuring that Richard was able to escape.[7]

It was about this time that Richard first tried to negotiate with his Muslim enemies. He sent a messenger to Saladin in an attempt to open diplomatic talks. Saladin sent his brother, Saif ad-Din al-Adil, to meet with Richard and be the go-between in the negotiations between the two leaders.

At first, Richard demanded three conditions for a settlement: control of Jerusalem, control of all the land between the Mediterranean coast and the Jordan River, and the return of the True Cross. Saladin rejected all three.

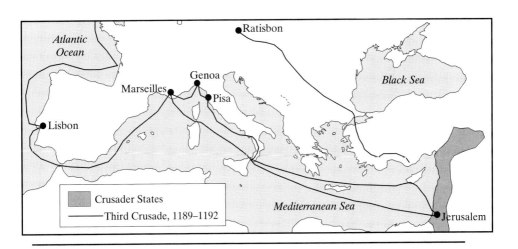

The Third Crusade owed most of its success to the leadership ability of Richard I, who, despite his many defeats of the Muslim army, knew that he could not defeat the city of Jerusalem.

Richard's next offer involved having his sister Joan marry Saif ad-Din. Although Saladin was not sure Richard was serious about this, he accepted the proposal as a basis for further negotiation. However, Joan upset her brother's plan when she refused to marry Saif ad-Din unless he became a Christian. This put an end to the round of negotiations.

By the end of 1191, Richard controlled the coast from Tyre, just north of Acre, to Jaffa. His last objective was to capture the fortress of Ascalon on the coast south of Jaffa. As he had done at Jaffa, Saladin destroyed the fortress of Ascalon and abandoned it to the Christians. Although Richard was unaware of the situation, Saladin was having political trouble within the alliance of Muslims maintaining support for his army in the Holy Land. Although Jerusalem was important to Muslims as the place where the prophet Mohammed was reported to have ascended to heaven, many Muslims at the time lacked the religious zeal of the Christian crusaders over the possession of the city. Mecca, in present-day Saudi Arabia, was—and still is—the most important place for Muslims. Had the battles been over Mecca the Muslims would most likely have matched the Christians' religious fervor. At Ascalon, however, Saladin retreated to Jerusalem to play a waiting game with Richard and his crusaders.[8]

The Politics of Crusading

Richard directed the reconstruction of the fortress of Ascalon. Now his position on the coast was solidified.

All that remained was to capture Jerusalem to make the Third Crusade an overwhelming success. As much as Richard may have wanted to recapture Jerusalem, events were preventing that from happening.

One of the major obstacles to further success was the quarreling among the various factions within the Christian army. The Christians who had ruled the Holy Land before Saladin had driven them out were divided into two major factions based on a number of issues, including who would rule in the Holy Land after they had finished reconquering it. Guy of Lusignan and Conrad of Monferrat led the two factions. The soldiers in Richard's army were torn between these leaders. Richard's crusaders represented every country in Europe. It has been estimated that Richard's soldiers spoke over twenty different languages.

To further complicate the situation, Richard received reports from home that his brother Prince John was plotting with King Philip II of France to take over Richard's position as king of England. Richard was first and foremost a soldier. He seemed to dislike the intrigues of twelfth-century politics, both at home and in the Holy Land. He knew that he might have to leave the Holy Land sooner than planned to deal with his problems at home.

Richard felt strongly that Guy of Lusignan, the former king of Jerusalem who had led the siege of Acre, should become the ruler of the Christian holdings in the Holy Land. Many others felt Conrad of Monferrat, another Christian leader of the Holy Land, had a better claim.

In an effort to settle this dispute, Richard called all the quarreling parties together at Ascalon on April 16, 1192. He let those present at the council choose. His role as the head of the Third Crusade depended on the support of those under him. Richard felt he could best keep his forces together by giving the various nobles in his council a say in who was to rule once he went back to Europe. They overwhelmingly gave their support to Conrad. Richard saw their decision as a slap in the face. As a consolation, Richard granted Guy the right to rule Cyprus.[9]

After he had conquered Cyprus on his way to the Holy Land, Richard had put his companions Richard de Canvil and Robert of Turnham in charge of the island. They immediately had problems controlling the local population. To rid himself of these problems, Richard had made a deal with the Templars to rule Cyprus. He sold them the rights to govern Cyprus for one hundred thousand dinars (currency). The Templars paid Richard forty thousand dinars immediately and were supposed to pay the rest from money they made running the island.

The Templars found the same problems that Richard's people had. The Muslim people of Cyprus were in constant revolt and required more attention than the Templars were willing to give. The Templars agreed to turn the island over to Guy of Lusignan if he would pay them forty thousand dinars. This would make up for the money they had given Richard. Guy quickly raised the money. He also agreed to pay the other sixty thousand dinars the Templars owed Richard. Many of the soldiers who had spent the last five years fighting with Guy in the Holy Land went to Cyprus with him. With their help, Guy was able to control the local population. Guy's family would rule Cyprus for almost two hundred years.[10]

Meanwhile, Conrad of Monferrat, the new leader of the Christian holdings in the Holy Land, quickly wed Queen Isabella of Jerusalem. Isabella had married the king of Jerusalem, Humphrey of Toron, when she was only eleven. Isabella was the daughter of Amalric I, who had also been king of Jerusalem. Isabella's marriage to Humphrey was declared void, and she married Conrad, who was made ruler of Jerusalem. However, Conrad's reign was short-lived. He was assassinated twelve days later on April 28. There were many suspects—a lot of angry people had been opposed to Conrad's election. Some even accused Richard of arranging the assassination, but many thought that the followers of Rashid ed-Din Sinan had assassinated Conrad. Rashid was the leader of a fanatical Muslim sect.

Henry of Champagne, who was a nephew of Richard's and was also related to Philip II, quickly succeeded Conrad. Although she protested at first, Henry also married Isabella. Although Henry was named king of Jerusalem, the crusaders would never actually succeed in conquering the city. They would have to

Source Document

This is, I say, a new kind of knighthood and one unknown to the ages gone by. It ceaselessly wages a twofold war both against flesh and blood and against a spiritual army of evil in the heavens. When someone strongly resists a foe in the flesh, relying solely on the strength of the flesh, I would hardly remark it, since this is common enough. And when war is waged by spiritual strength against vices or demons, this, too, is nothing remarkable, praiseworthy as it is, for the world is full of monks. But when the one sees a man powerfully girding himself with both swords and nobly marking his belt, who would not consider it worthy of all wonder, the more so since it has been hitherto unknown? He is truly a fearless knight and secure on every side, for his soul is protected by the armor of faith just as his body is protected by armor of steel. He is thus doubly armed and need fear neither demons nor men. Not that he fears death—no, he desires it. Why should he fear to live or fear to die when for him to live is Christ, and to die is gain? Gladly and faithfully he stands for Christ, but he would prefer to be dissolved and to be with Christ, by far the better thing.[11]

This account of the new Knights of Templar was given by Bernard of Clairvaux.

be satisfied with holding on to the cities they had captured along the coast.

The Final Battles

Richard knew that, even if he captured Jerusalem, he could not hold it.[12] There were just too many Muslims, and Jerusalem was too far from the coast to keep supplied. Despite this, Richard wanted to finish his work along the coast.

The only remaining Muslim outpost on the coast was at Darum (southwest of Jerusalem). Richard arrived there on May 17, 1192. He was confronted with an impressive fortress with seventeen towers, thick walls, and a deep ditch. It was time once again to put his siege equipment to work.

Richard was in such a rush to get the siege started that he and his knights helped the regular soldiers and sailors move equipment from the landing site to the fortress. Richard is said to have carried one large and heavy piece of equipment all by himself for over a mile without even breaking a sweat.[13]

Richard and his men set up their siege weapons and then kept them firing around the clock. Five days after the bombardment started, the defenders of Darum offered to give up the fortress if Richard would let them leave unharmed. Richard would not make a deal. Richard knew he could capture Darum and those defending it. He did not want to turn the Muslim troops free and let them join with Saladin. Richard continued the siege with a plan to use sappers.

Sappers were special workers who could tunnel under walls and weaken them so they would collapse. At Darum, the sappers dug under one of the towers. When they had weakened it, Richard turned the full force of the bombardment on that one tower. It soon cracked and came crashing down, leaving a huge gap in the wall.

Richard and his soldiers rushed into Darum. The defenders fell back to the largest and tallest tower in the fortress. When Richard had taken control of the rest of the town, he turned his attention to the final tower. The defenders in it surrendered unconditionally. Had they known what was in store for them, they might have fought until they all died in battle. Richard's men threw many of them off the tower and left them lying on the ground below to die. Other prisoners were beheaded or had their throats slit. Those who were not killed were locked in chains and later sold into slavery. With Darum defeated, Richard and the Christians now had full control of the coast and a strong position from which to negotiate with Saladin.[14]

On Jerusalem's Doorstep

After the defeat of Darum, Richard spent a month encamped at Beit Nuba, just thirteen miles from Jerusalem. Here he tried to bring together all the remaining crusaders who had spread out along the coast. While he waited, he raided Saladin's supply lines. Richard's most successful raid was against an armed caravan coming to Jerusalem from Egypt. He led the

Many of the crusaders were genuinely inspired by religious fervor. Upon seeing the Holy City of Jerusalem for the first time, many of the Christian soldiers openly wept.

raid personally and was in the thick of the fighting when he and his men surprised the caravan at dawn on June 23, 1192. The raid brought a huge quantity of supplies and treasure to Richard and his army. There were thousands of mules, horses, and camels, as well as food, cloth, and weapons.[15] It appeared that the time was finally right to attack Jerusalem.

Richard had made several attempts to approach Jerusalem in the past. Knowing he could not maintain a long siege of the city, however, he had withdrawn each time. On one of these attempts, he got close enough to the city to see its towers. It is reported that rather than look at the Holy City, Richard covered his eyes and said, "Sweet Lord, I entreat Thee, do not suffer me to see Thy Holy City, since I am unable to deliver it from the hands of Thine enemies!"[16]

At this point, Richard probably could have taken the city, but he knew that, once he left, the forces he left behind would never be able to hold it. Richard decided that, strategically, it was more important to hold on to as much of the coast as possible.

Many in the crusading army were very disappointed. They pledged to stay and capture Jerusalem even if Richard left. Some of the remaining French soldiers supposedly made up songs making fun of Richard's inability to accomplish the final goal of the Crusade. However, Richard was wise enough to know what he was able to accomplish. He also knew it was time to go home while he still had a home to return to.[17]

The Crusades were fought, in part, in order to keep such sites as the Holy Sepulcher open for Christian pilgrims from Europe to visit.

Richard's Last Days in the Holy Land

As much as Richard wanted to go back to Europe, at this point he could not leave without at least ensuring that Christian pilgrims would be able to visit Jerusalem. Since a military solution was unlikely, Richard returned to negotiations with Saladin.

During the negotiations, Saladin attacked Jaffa. Richard was so angry that he quickly boarded a ship in Acre with eighty knights and four hundred archers and sailed for Jaffa. It was in this battle that Richard showed his great strength as a military tactician. Despite his tiny force of knights, as the Muslims attacked, Richard held his archers in reserve and proceeded to fight an organized retreat. Just as it appeared that Saladin's forces would take the city, Richard's archers fired arrows at the tightly packed Muslims, forcing them to retreat. Once again, Saladin saw the power of the European military.

Richard and Saladin Agree to a Peace Treaty

After the successful defense of Jaffa, both Richard and Saladin were ready to negotiate a settlement to the conflict. The final terms of the peace called for a three-year truce between the crusaders and the Muslims. The Christians would keep the entire coast from Tyre to Jaffa, while Ascalon would go back to the Muslims. During the years of the truce, unarmed pilgrims would have free access to Jerusalem and the nearby holy sites in Bethlehem and Nazareth. Richard

Source Document

Saladin allowed Joppa to be restored to the Christians. They were to occupy the city and its vicinity, including the seacoast and the mountains, freely and quietly. Saladin agreed to confirm an inviolate peace between Christians and Saracens, guaranteeing for both free passage and access to the Holy Sepulcher of the Lord without the exaction of any tribute and with the freedom of bringing objects for sale through any land whatever and of exercising a free commerce. When these conditions of peace had been reduced to writing and read to him, King Richard agreed to observe them, for he could not hope for anything much better, especially since he was sick, relying upon scanty support, and was not more than two miles from the enemy's station. Whoever contends that Richard should have felt otherwise about this peace agreement should know that he thereby marks himself as a perverse liar.[18]

After deciding that he could not hold Jerusalem, Richard used his position of strength to make a peace with Saladin that would allow Christians to continue to make pilgrimages to the Holy Land.

and Saladin signed the treaty on September 2, 1192, bringing to an end the Third Crusade.[19]

To celebrate the peace, Richard and his followers held a huge feast and a tournament at Jaffa. During the celebration, Richard sent a note to Saladin saying that he would be back at the end of the truce to capture Jerusalem. Saladin replied that, if he had to lose land, he would rather lose it to Richard than to any other person.

Richard spent the next month preparing for his departure. He set sail from Acre for Europe on October 9, 1192.[20]

Chapter 9

The Trip Home

Travel in the twelfth century was always perilous, even for the ruler of England and half of France. Richard's original plan had been to sail to Marseilles, France, and then make the short journey overland to his lands in France. Somehow, Richard learned that Raymond of Toulouse, his rival and former enemy, was planning to try to capture him between Marseilles and home. Apparently, Raymond felt he still had a score to settle with Richard. So, Richard changed his plans. He would change the course of his journey and also disguise himself as a poor Christian pilgrim, to avoid being noticed by his enemies. During a stop at Corfu, one of the Greek islands, Richard struck a deal with some pirates to have him and twenty of his followers transported up the Adriatic Sea (the body of water between the Ionian and Italian peninsulas). Richard most likely planned to land at Venice, Italy. However, a storm sent them off course and they landed instead at Ragusa on the island of Sicily.

From Ragusa, they headed east and then north up the Adriatic. Richard found it hard to act like a poor pilgrim. He and his grouped stayed in the best inns and spent large sums of money for food and entertainment.

The group sailed farther up the Adriatic in December 1192, until a storm struck. The ship they were on was damaged and forced them ashore on the Istria peninsula in present-day Croatia near the northern end of the Adriatic Sea.

Once on land, Richard decided that it might be better if someone else appeared to be in charge of the group. Baldwin of Béthune acted as leader, and Richard posed as a merchant traveling with him. However, by this time, word had spread that Richard was in Europe traveling in disguise. Many people were looking for him.

In addition to his worries of being captured by Raymond of Toulouse, this new route took Richard through the lands of Duke Leopold of Austria. Leopold was the same person Richard had humiliated during the Crusade by allowing his flag to be torn down after the Christian victory at Acre. Leopold was eager to get back at Richard.

The duke's followers discovered that Richard was in their territory when one of Richard's servants spent a lot of money at a market in Vienna, Austria. It was immediately apparent that this group was made up of people who were much more than regular soldiers and pilgrims returning from the Holy Land. When the duke learned that Richard was within his grasp, he had Richard and his followers arrested and locked up in a castle at Durrenstein, about forty-five miles from Vienna. Leopold was so concerned about keeping Richard in his midst, that he had those guarding him keep their swords drawn at all times.[1]

Richard Held for Ransom

Once Leopold had Richard as a captive, he had to decide what to do with him. Part of Leopold's anger over Acre had to do with the fact that he was cut out from receiving a share of the plunder when Acre fell. He saw Richard's capture as a way to make up for the loss he felt he had experienced at Acre. Leopold, therefore, demanded that Richard pay a huge ransom to be released.

The Roman Catholic Church had ordered that crusaders were to have free passage throughout Christian lands. However, Richard had made many enemies during the Crusade, such as Phillip II of France and Richard's own brother Prince John, who wanted to rule England. These enemies were willing to pay Leopold to keep Richard prisoner for as long as possible. Although Richard's European allies knew he had been captured, they did not know exactly where he was being held.

Early in 1193, Richard was moved to the court of the Holy Roman emperor, Henry VI, at Regensburg (northeast of present-day Munich, Germany). After consulting with Henry, Leopold demanded as ransom the equivalent of one hundred fifty thousand marks (a common currency), which would have been thirty-five tons of silver. The two leaders agreed in advance that they would split the ransom. At today's silver prices, the ransom would be worth about $5.8 million. Silver was even more valuable during Richard's time.

By now, Prince John was in league with the French. He had pledged his loyalty to King Philip II for the lands that Richard had held in France. Some even suggested that John had also promised that England would acknowledge the French king as their ruler in the future. John needed a strong ally if he were going to defy his brother Richard successfully. Philip was his obvious ally, since John had holdings in France, as did many other members of the English nobility. Considering his position with the French, it is not surprising that Prince John put little effort into raising the ransom for his brother.

The task of raising the ransom fell to Richard's mother, Eleanor of Aquitaine, and the people of England who were still loyal to Richard. It seemed that Richard's English subjects were more willing to help pay for his return than they were to support Prince John. Despite Richard's continuing popularity, it still took over a year for Eleanor to raise the ransom, considering she had no legal authority to raise money from the people. A one-time direct tax was enacted to raise the ransom. Everyone had to pay a tax equivalent to 25 percent of his or her annual income. In addition to this early form of income tax, all the churches were required to donate their gold and silver altar decorations to the ransom. Churches that did not have any gold or silver were required to pay an amount equal to 25 percent of the year's wool production. Wool was the major cash crop and trade good of England at the time.

In January 1194, Eleanor set out for Germany with the ransom. Richard was finally set free on February 4, 1194. This was the first time Richard and Eleanor had seen each other since Eleanor had brought Berengaria to meet her future husband in Messina at the beginning of the Third Crusade.

On March 13, 1194, Richard I, king of England and leader of the Third Crusade, returned to England for the first time since his departure for the Crusades in 1190. His first stop was at a religious shrine in Canterbury, where Richard gave thanks for his successful return. On March 23, 1194, Richard triumphantly rode into London with his mother riding in a place of honor at his side.

Putting the Pieces Back Together

Prince John and his supporters in England and France had done much to undermine Richard's rule while he was in the Holy Land and during his captivity in Germany. Richard would spend the rest of his life trying to put the pieces back together. At the time of Richard's return, Prince John was keeping a low profile in one of his French castles. The barons who had been loyal to John quickly surrendered their castles to Richard without resistance—with one exception. At Nottingham, Prince John's followers were determined to resist the king. Their resolve to defend their castle disappeared when they learned that Richard was personally going to lead the attack. When Richard arrived, the defenders of the castle quickly surrendered. The stories of Richard's feats in the Holy Land had arrived home before him. Despite their loyalty to Prince John, the defenders of Nottingham Castle did not want to become the victims of another of Richard's military victories.

It is at this point that history and myth come together in a part of the story that may never be proven one way or the other. Some have reported that after Nottingham Castle surrendered to the king and his army, there was a meeting between Robin Hood and King Richard the Lionhearted. Historians are still debating the existence of a real Robin Hood. Many believe he was a crusading knight who had been to the Holy Land with Richard and returned home to find his lands confiscated by Prince John. Legends claim that this knight joined up with peasants who had fled to the forest to avoid persecution by John's tax collectors. Whether there was a real Robin Hood or not, many agree that Prince John's harsh treatment of the peasants caused many to become outlaws living in the woods of England. It is also a fact that, during Richard's absence, members of the nobility who refused to follow Prince John often lost their lands. Those who opposed John remained loyal to their crusading king. Some have reported that, after the surrender of Nottingham Castle, Richard gave Robin Hood and his men a full pardon for any crimes with which Prince John's officials might have charged them. In the years that followed, the stories of Robin Hood grew, making him a central character in the stories about the time.[2]

With the surrender of Nottingham Castle, the supporters of Prince John were removed from their official positions. Richard was once again the undisputed king of England. One of his first acts was to revoke all the charters he had sold to government officials in 1189, and sell them back. As always, Richard needed money to support his next military exploits. This time, however, he would be traveling only across the English Channel. He would spend the rest of his life fighting for the lands in France that King Philip II of France, his brother John, and other nobles had taken from him while he was away on the Third Crusade.[3]

Richard left England in May 1194, after a stay of only three months. He would never return. It is interesting to note that Richard I is considered an important English king, despite the fact that he never spent much time there. The impact of his reign was a product of the changing times of the Middle Ages. The growth and power of towns and the growing importance of trade were, in part, due to Richard's successes in the Holy Land. The fact that Richard was gone so much allowed England the chance to grow and expand without a lot of government interference.

Richard Reestablishes Control

As soon as Richard returned to his lands in France, Prince John came to him, seeking forgiveness. Just as their father had forgiven them for their plots against him, Richard quickly forgave his brother for all he had done. Richard had always been fond of his younger brother, and the importance of family alliances outweighed all Prince John's plotting. From this point on, John became one of Richard's strongest supporters in his battles to regain his lands from French King Philip II.

Richard had learned much about warfare during his Crusade in the Holy Land. He quickly put his new knowledge to work. Richard had always been fascinated with buildings, and he proved to be as good at designing and building them as he had been in the Holy Land at defeating and destroying them.

In France, he needed to have a strong base from which he could recapture his lost lands. He picked a spot high on a cliff overlooking the Seine River, at Les Andelys. There, he built a fortress known as Château Gaillard. It took Richard just over a year to build the fortress, which had none of the decorative aspects used for castles of the time. However, using the information he had learned during the Crusade, he built a formidable base that would be almost impossible to capture.

With his brother Prince John at his side and his lands in Normandy defended by Château Gaillard, Richard could turn his attention to regaining the lands Philip II had taken while Richard was in the Holy Land. The warfare that followed between the two was in some ways similar to Richard's crusading efforts. Philip's armies were no match for Richard's in large-scale battles, but Richard and his forces were able to prolong the war through sieges of his smaller holdings and through surprise attacks. With his military superiority, Richard was eventually able to regain all the lands he lost. He then turned his attentions to expanding his holdings into Philip's territory.

The war between Richard and Philip affected the politics of all of Europe. Other leaders allied themselves with one side or the other. Many who had been Philip's supporters ended up siding with Richard. They now feared that Philip might become too powerful if he defeated Richard. Although Richard might have been able to defeat Philip, he was stopped by an age-old problem. In the ten years that he had been king, huge sums of money had been raised on Richard's behalf: first for the Crusade, then for his ransom, and finally, for the campaign against Philip. Hubert Walter, the person Richard had left in charge of England, asserted that 1.1 million marks had been sent to Richard during his four-year war against Philip, the equivalent of $42.5 million today. By 1198, Richard was running out of funds. He was forced, as he had been with Saladin, to seek an end to the war with Philip through a treaty.[4]

Treaty With Philip II

On January 13, 1199, Richard and Philip II signed a peace treaty that was intended to last for five years. Their lack of trust for each other was apparent even at the signing of the treaty. Richard arrived by boat while Philip came on horseback. During their meeting, Richard stayed in the relative safety of his boat. Documents the two kings had to sign were ferried back and forth. The treaty gave each king the right to all lands that he currently held and created an uneasy situation in which neither king had the advantage.[5]

At this point, Richard was thinking about his unfinished business in the Holy Land and the possibility of another Crusade. Richard was first and foremost a warrior king. With peace at home, there would be little for him to do. The day-to-day governing of his lands had always been the responsibility of his nobility and the growing class of government officials. The changing nature of commerce and government was creating a new class of citizens. These were civil servants who worked in the business of government.

As Richard thought about his future, word came that one of his subjects, Archard of Châlus, had recently gained possession of a large treasure. The story goes that one of the peasants of Châlus was plowing a field next to the castle when he discovered a treasure of gold and silver figurines and coins. Most historians believe that the coins were Roman and may have been buried in the fifth century during the last days of the Roman Empire.[6] Richard's greed got the better of him, and he demanded that all the treasure be turned over to him. He immediately set out to Châlus with his army. When Archard refused to hand over the treasure, Richard decided to lay siege to his castle. On March 26, 1199, Richard and some of his men rode around the castle, studying its defenses and planning their attack.

As Richard approached, Bertrand de Gourdon, one of the soldiers defending the castle, fired an arrow that hit Richard in the shoulder. It was not a serious wound. However, when Richard tried to pull out the arrow himself, he broke the shaft and left the arrowhead in his shoulder. There was nothing to do but have one of the army's surgeons cut out the arrowhead. Although the operation was successful, the wound became infected. As was often the case for soldiers of the time, this nonthreatening wound became a fatal infection known as gangrene. As gangrene festered in his shoulder, Richard knew he was dying and sent word to his mother. Eleanor rushed to the side of her dying son.

Richard's men knew their king was dying and sought to avenge his death. They attacked the castle of Châlus with all their fury and quickly destroyed it. In the process of destroying the castle, they killed everyone inside except the fateful crossbowman, Bertrand de Gourdon. The saddened warriors brought Bertrand before their dying king. Richard raised himself and asked Bertrand, "What harm have I done you, that you have killed me?"[7]

Bertrand responded that Richard had killed his father and two brothers in battle, most likely the attack on the castle then being fought. Bertrand showed no remorse for what he had done to Richard. He stated to the king that he would gladly undergo any torture that could be devised as long as he was the one responsible for Richard's death. Richard responded by forgiving Bertrand and granting him his freedom.

Richard's men, however, did not feel the same way. If Bertrand were willing to be tortured for what he had done to their king, they would gladly oblige him. Mercadier, a French mercenary who had been with Richard throughout the Crusade, was now the head of Richard's army. He sent Bertrand to Joan of Toulouse, Richard's sister, who devised a fitting torture for the defiant Bertrand. First, he was blinded; then his skin was beaten off his body with a stick while he was still alive. Finally, he was bound to two horses that were sent off in opposite directions, tearing his body apart.

With his mother, Eleanor, who was now close to eighty, at his side, Richard the Lionhearted made his final preparations for the ascent to heaven he believed he had earned as a crusader. He gave all his titles and lands to his brother John, along with three quarters of all of his treasure. The remaining quarter was to be distributed to the poor among his subjects. The royal jewels were left to his nephew, Otto of Brunswick, who was emperor-elect of the Holy Roman Empire. Richard made his final confession and received last rites, a Roman Catholic tradition that reportedly prepares the soul for entry into heaven. He succumbed to the infection and died on April 6, 1199, at the age of forty-one. Richard's last request was that his blood, brain, and intestines be buried at Châlus. He asked that his heart be buried at Rouen, and his body buried next to his father, Henry II, at Fontevrault on the Loire River in the French province of Anjou.[8]

These burial requests may seem bizarre, but Richard had his reasons. During his last rites, he confessed that he had betrayed his father to Philip II of France and wanted his body buried at his father's feet as a final act of contrition. Richard wanted his heart buried at Rouen because of the support he had received from, and the love he felt for, the people of that city. His internal organs went to Châlus in Poitou because Richard felt that was all they deserved.

Chapter 10

The Legacy of Richard and the Later Crusades

The First Crusade had opened trade between Europe and the Middle East. However, if Richard had not successfully reestablished the Christian holdings along the coast, that trade might have ended. The fall of Jerusalem in 1187, when control of the entire region went to Saladin and his Turkish armies, might have prevented Europe from growing and prospering.

Trade with the Middle East was critical to the explosion of wealth and prosperity in Europe. Without it, all of Europe would have found it difficult to get past the period many historians have called the Dark Ages. Much of the knowledge that had been lost after the fall of the Roman Empire had been maintained and added to in the libraries and schools of the Muslims and Eastern Orthodox Christians. In part because of the Crusades, this knowledge in science, medicine, and the arts made its way to Europe, along with the other riches of the Middle and Far East. Richard's reestablishment of a European presence in the Middle East was one of the factors that helped bring an end to the Dark Ages in Europe.

Beyond the importance of the exchange of goods and ideas with the Middle East, Richard's rule was important to England for other reasons. It is important to remember that Richard's great-great-grandfather, William the Conqueror, had crossed the English Channel from Normandy in 1066 and taken over the country. By the time of Richard's reign, many of the Norman families that had been given lands by William had, in many ways, become English. As time went on, and especially during Richard's absences, the English nobility became more independent. They began to see England as an independent country. At the same time, the ties between the English nobility and its Norman French relatives grew more distant. The unpopularity of Prince John among the English made these differences even greater. By the time Richard died and John became king, the English nobility wanted more control over England. They rebelled against King John. The rebellion led to one of the most important events in English and later United States history.

To settle his problems with the English barons, King John agreed to the Magna Carta in 1215. This is the first historical document that limited the powers of the king and established a rule of law that applied to all. This document became the foundation for the

Source Document

1. In the first place we have granted to God, and by this our present charter confirmed for us and our heirs for ever that the English church shall be free, and shall have her rights entire, and her liberties inviolate; . . . We have also granted to all freemen of our kingdom, for us and our heirs for ever, all the underwritten liberties, to be had and held by them and their heirs, of us and our heirs for ever. . . .

9. Neither we nor our bailiffs shall seize any land or rent for any debt, so long as the chattels of the debtor are sufficient to repay the debt; nor shall the sureties of the debtor be distrained so long as the principal debtor is able to satisfy the debt. . . .

13. And the city of London shall have all its ancient liberties and freecustoms, as well by land as by water; furthermore, we decree and grant that all other cities, boroughs, towns, and ports shall have all their liberties and free customs.[1]

The most important aspect of King John's reign was perhaps his acceptance of the Magna Carta, the document that serves as the basis for the civil rights of both the English and the Americans.

English parliamentary system of government. The concept that the government must answer to the people, instead of the other way around, is the idea that the American patriots called on when they declared their independence from England and created the United States.

The Fourth Crusade

The Third Crusade was the last great victory for Christianity. Although there were a number of other campaigns that were called Crusades by their leaders, their motives and objectives were often questionable.

As the emerging nations of Europe gained economic and political power, the power of the Roman Catholic Church diminished. The failure of the Third Crusade to capture Jerusalem also reflected negatively on the Church. When Innocent III became pope in 1198, he called for a new Crusade as a way to regain some of the glory and power the Church had lost. Those who were willing to answer the call for the Fourth Crusade had personal objectives that had little to do with earlier crusading objectives in the Holy Land.

German Duke Philip of Swabia and his cousin Boniface of Monferrat were concerned about the political situation in Constantinople. Constantinople was the capital of the Byzantine Empire and the center of the Eastern Orthodox Church. Since the rise in power of the Turks, the Byzantine Emperors had become allies of the West. Philip's brother-in-law,

Alexius, was the heir to the throne of Byzantine Emperor Isaac Comnenus. However, Comnenus had been overthrown. In 1204, Philip and Boniface led an army into Constantinople, planning to put Alexius on the Byzantine throne. The soldiers from the West captured the city. Problems began as the army sacked the city. They robbed and defiled holy sites and killed much of the population.

The sack of Constantinople shocked the pope. Since the end of the Roman Empire there had been problems between the two branches of Christianity. The earlier Crusades had offered hope that the two Churches would settle their differences. The Fourth Crusade ended any hope of the two sides working together. In fact, the rift between the two factions of Christianity still exists to this day.

The Byzantine Empire had existed for almost nine hundred years. However, the sacking of Constantinople weakened the Byzantines to such a point that the Turks eventually took over and eventually created the modern country of Turkey two-hundred-fifty years later. So, rather than further the cause of Christianity, this Crusade did just the opposite.[2]

The Children's Crusade

The next Crusade, the Children's Crusade, was a disaster of another type. In 1212, a French shepherd boy named Stephen claimed he had a vision. In a dream, he said Jesus Christ came to him and told him to raise an army and lead it to the Holy Land. Thousands of

The Children's Crusade, in which thousands of young Europeans ended up dead or sold into slavery, was one of the saddest events in the history of the Crusades.

children and adults followed Stephen to the south of France, where most of the children were captured by slave traders and taken to Egypt.

Another boy, named Nicholas, who lived near Cologne (on the Rhine River in Germany), raised an army of fifty thousand children and marched south over the Alps to Italy. Those who did not die of illness

Source Document

In this year occurred an outstanding thing and one much to be marveled at, for it is unheard of throughout the ages. About the time of Easter and Pentecost, without anyone having preached or called for it and prompted by I know not what spirit, many thousands of boys, ranging in age from six years to full maturity, left the plows or carts which they were driving, the flocks which they were pasturing, and anything else which they were doing. This they did despite the wishes of their parents, relatives, and friends who sought to make them draw back. Suddenly one ran after another to take the cross. Thus, by groups of twenty, or fifty, or a hundred, they put up banners and began to journey to Jerusalem.[3]

A contemporary historian gave this account of the devastating Children's Crusade in 1212.

or starvation ended up in the hands of slave traders and disappeared.[4]

The Fifth Crusade

In 1218, Pope Innocent III declared an end to feudal war in Europe. Any noblemen who continued to fight each other for control of territory would be excommunicated from the Church. Excommunication was taken seriously by the people of the Middle Ages, who believed that the Church controlled access to heaven. So, rather than fight among themselves in Europe, a number of campaigns to the Holy Land were attempted.

Duke Leopold of Austria and King Andrew of Hungary led the Fifth Crusade. They set out with no real plan in mind but thought they might attack Egypt. The sultan of Egypt, Al-Adil, the brother of Saladin (who had died in 1193), refused to fight them. After wandering around in the desert for a while, the Christian army arrived in Acre. The Christians who were in control of Acre were not happy to see them. They had been living peacefully with their Muslim neighbors and did not want to start any trouble. In their wanderings, the crusaders claimed to have found an earthen pot that Jesus had used to change water into wine at a wedding feast. Their discovery was never verified.

The Sixth Crusade

The Sixth Crusade was even less noble. Emperor Frederic of Germany had married the daughter of John of Brienne, who was king of Jerusalem. When

John died in 1227, Frederic claimed his title and planned a Crusade to obtain it. The pope disagreed with his claim and went as far as excommunicating Frederic in an attempt to stop him from taking an army to the Holy Land. Frederic ignored the pope and landed in the Holy Land on February 18, 1229.

The Muslims who lived in peace with the Christians of the Holy Land were concerned about who ruled them. They agreed with Frederic's claim and granted him control of the coastal cities and the three holy cities of Jerusalem, Bethlehem, and Nazareth. The Christians of the area were unhappy about having an excommunicated king. However, neither side really needed to worry. Frederic returned to Europe after only a month in the Holy Land. He retained the title of king of Jerusalem in name only. For the next fifteen years, a state of anarchy existed in much of the Holy Land.

The Seventh and Eighth Crusades

In 1244, a group of Turkish fanatics, known as Mamelukes, attacked Jerusalem. The Mamelukes destroyed much of the city. Again, the people of Europe were upset by attacks on the Christian holy places. French King Louis IX came forward to lead the Seventh Crusade.

King Louis IX, like some of his predecessors in the earlier crusades, was a very religious man. He went to the Holy Land with good intentions. Unfortunately, his military ability did not match his religious feelings.

The later Crusades were often fought not for religious reasons but for wealth and profit. French King Louis IX on horseback was one of the few later crusaders whose religious sentiments were genuine.

In a poorly planned campaign against the Egyptian city of Mansourah, Louis's brother attacked without orders, splitting up the Christian force. Rather than taking over what should have been a rather easy target, Louis and thousands of his knights were captured.

The remaining crusaders were forced to pay a huge ransom for Louis's release. After he was set free, he spent four more years in the Holy Land. During this time, he helped the Christians in the area build up their defenses. It is reported that Louis liked the Holy Land very much. He might have stayed even longer had he not been called back to attend to matters in France in 1254.

Louis tried to return to the Holy Land in 1270. He got as far as Carthage (an ancient city located in modern Tunisia). Here, King Louis IX came down with a fever and died. It is reported that his last words were "Jerusalem, Jerusalem." It was a place he would never reach in this world.[5]

The End of Crusading

There were other campaigns in the Middle East over the next half-century, but none ever matched the success of the First Crusade or of Richard the Lionhearted's Third Crusade. The only one who came close to capturing the earlier zeal of the crusaders was King Louis IX, who led both the Seventh Crusade and the Eighth Crusade.

Since the twelfth and thirteenth centuries, the Holy Land has been a site of ongoing problems.

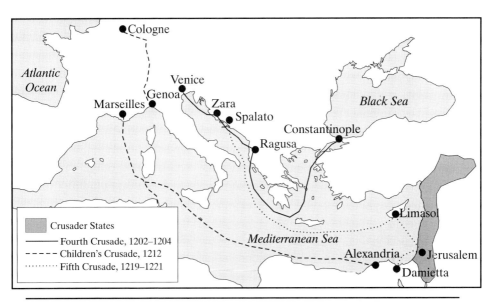

None of the many Crusades undertaken after Richard's Third Crusade was any more successful in winning back Christian control of key regions of the Holy Land.

Sailors of the fifteenth century needed to find a water route to the Orient because of continuing conflicts in the Middle East. The demand for goods from Asia had become so strong that great efforts were made to find a secure trade route that avoided the uncertainties of doing business in the Middle East. These ongoing problems between the different religious and ethnic groups of the Middle East frequently disrupted the trade with the countries of Asia that had become so important to Europe. After World War I, a number of European protectorates were established in the Middle East in an attempt to control the area, but tensions continued.

After the persecution of the Jews during World War II, a Jewish state was set up in the Holy Land, or Palestine, as it was called at that time. This area had been the historical homeland of the Jewish people. Many Muslims who lived in the area were driven out when Palestine became the modern Jewish state of Israel. Today, Europe and other countries, such as the United States, are still concerned about the security of the area. Tension still exists between the Jews of Israel and the Muslims who live both inside Israel and in the nearby Muslim countries of Egypt, Syria, Lebanon, and Iraq.

Jerusalem and the other Christian holy sites of the region remain extremely important. Hundreds of thousands of Christians still make pilgrimages to the Holy Land each year. Meanwhile, the Israelis and Muslims continue to try to settle some of their disputes. The Holy Land remains a point of concern and interest for the entire world.

Although Richard the Lionhearted never actually saw Jerusalem, his efforts and the efforts of other crusaders helped bring about profound changes in Europe and in the Middle East that are still felt today.

Timeline

1066—At the Battle of Hastings, William the Conqueror defeats the English and becomes king of England.

1071—At the Battle of Manzikert, Seljuk Turks defeat the Byzantine army; The Byzantines ask the West for help.

1095—Pope Urban II travels to Clermont, France, and makes a call for the First Crusade.

1096—The Paupers' Crusade arrives in the Holy Land and is decimated by the Turks.

1097—The armies of the First Crusade, also called the Barons' Crusade, arrive in Constantinople and begin their successful campaign to capture the Holy Land.

1099—*July 15*: Jerusalem is captured by the crusaders; Godfrey of Bouillon is named king of Jerusalem and begins eighty-eight years of Christian rule in Jerusalem.

1144—Turks recapture Edessa and other Christian strongholds along the land route to Jerusalem.

1145—The Second Crusade is launched, only to have the Christian forces humiliated by poor leadership and the superior forces of the Turks.

1153—The Muslim army captures Ascalon along the coast of Palestine and threatens the remaining Christians in the area.

1157—Richard the Lionhearted is born on September 8, the third son of King Henry II of England and Eleanor of Aquitaine.

1167—Richard's parents, Eleanor and Henry, separate; Richard moves with his mother to Aquitaine.

1172—Henry II names Richard duke of Aquitaine, but retains all real power over the area for himself.

1173—Richard begins a campaign against his father to assert his claim to Aquitaine and the surrounding lands.

1174—Henry II defeats his son's rebellion and then immediately pardons him; Henry assigns Richard the task of subduing some of his father's enemies in the area.

1183—Two of Richard's brothers, Henry the Younger and Geoffrey, die; Richard becomes heir to all his father's titles, including king of England.

1187—*July 4*: At the Battle of Hattin, Saladin, leader of the Muslim armies in the Holy Land, wins a major victory against the Christians.
October 2: Jerusalem falls to Saladin; The entire Western world is shocked at the news; Pope Urban III calls for another Crusade, and Richard is one of the first to volunteer.

1189—*July 6*: Henry II dies; Richard succeeds him.
September 1: Richard arrives in England to be crowned king; Almost immediately, Richard begins preparing to go on the Crusade.
December: Richard I leaves England for France to meet with Philip II.
Christians in the Holy Land begin the siege of Acre.

1190—Richard I, king of England, and Philip II, king of France, embark from Marseilles on the Third Crusade; Frederick Barbarossa, the Holy Roman emperor, also leaves for the Third Crusade but takes the overland route to Constantinople; Because of these three kings' involvement, the Third Crusade is often referred to as the Kings' Crusade.
June 10: Frederick Barbarossa drowns while crossing the Calycadnus River; Most of those in his army who go on are defeated by the Turks.

1191—Richard and his ships are blown off course on their way to the Holy Land, and his sister Joan and fiancée, Berengaria, are captured by the ruler of Cyprus; Rather than pay ransom, Richard captures Cyprus, which will be ruled by western Christians for four hundred years; Richard and Berengaria are married; First Philip and then Richard arrive at Acre on the coast of Palestine, which Christian forces had been besieging for three years; With the combined forces, Acre falls to the crusaders.
September 7: The Battle of Arsuf is fought. This is the first battle of the Third Crusade where the two armies meet in open warfare; The Christian army soundly defeats Saladin's army.

1192—During the siege of Jaffa, Richard captures the city, solidifying his hold on the coast of Palestine; Richard and Saladin come to a negotiated settlement where the Christians keep most of the coast of Palestine, and Saladin agrees to allow all unarmed Christian pilgrims access to Jerusalem and other holy sites;. The final treaty is signed on September 2.
October 9: Richard leaves Palestine and heads home to attempt to settle the problems created by his brother Prince John and Philip II of France.
December: After changing routes and being transported by pirates, Richard and a small group of followers are captured by Duke Leopold of Austria and held for ransom.

1193—Due to the costs of the Crusade, Richard's followers in England, led by his mother, have difficulty raising the ransom of one hundred fifty thousand marks.

1194—*February 4*: Eleanor of Aquitaine arrives in Germany, pays the ransom, and Richard is set free.
March 13: Richard returns to England where he receives a hero's welcome; Richard quickly takes

care of those nobles who were loyal to his brother and resistant to his return as king.

May: Richard leaves England for the last time as he heads to France to regain his holdings there.

January 13: Richard and Philip II of France sign a treaty ending their prolonged war over Richard's lands in France.

1199—*March 26*: Richard is wounded by a single crossbow arrow while scouting the castle at Châlus, which he was planning to attack; Although the wound itself is not life threatening, it becomes infected and Richard dies on April 6.

1204—The Fourth Crusade sacks Constantinople.

1212—The Children's Crusade fails to reach the Holy Land and most participants either die or are captured by slave traders.

1219—The Fifth Crusade attacks Egypt and succeeds in capturing Damietta, a port city on the Nile River delta; Turks recapture it in 1221.

1229—The Sixth Crusade, led by Holy Roman Emperor Frederick II briefly regains control of Jerusalem.

1248—The Seventh Crusade begins under the direction of King Louis IX of France.

1249—King Louis recaptures Damietta and marches on toward Cairo.

1250—King Louis's army is totally defeated at the Battle of Mansourah; Many of those captured are slaughtered, and Louis is held for ransom.

1254—King Louis agrees to pay a ransom of eight hundred thousand gold pieces and return Damietta in exchange for his freedom.

1270—King Louis IX dies of plague in Carthage while leading the Eighth Crusade against the Muslims in North Africa.

Chapter Notes

Chapter 1. Rescuing Jaffa

1. John Matthews and Bob Stewart, *Warriors of Medieval Times* (Poole, Dorset, England: Firebird, 1993), p. 174.

Chapter 2. The Middle Ages and the Crusades

1. Oliver J. Thatcher and Edgar Holmes McNeal, eds., *A Source Book for Medieval History* (New York: Scribner's, 1905), pp. 513–517.

Chapter 3. Richard the Lionhearted

1. James A. Brundage, *Richard Lion Heart* (New York: Scribner's, 1974), pp. 25–28.

2. Philip Henderson, *Richard Coeur de Lion: A Biography* (New York: Norton, 1959), pp. 45–46.

3. Brundage, pp. 39–40.

4. Henderson, pp. 51–52.

5. Brundage, pp. 55–61.

6. Henderson, pp. 73–74.

Chapter 4. Life in the Middle Ages

1. J.F.C. Harrison, *The Common People of Great Britain: A History from the Norman Conquest to the Present* (Bloomington: Indiana University Press, 1985), pp. 45–47.

2. G. O. Sayles, *The Medieval Foundations of England* (New York: Barnes, 1961), pp. 224–233.

3. C. Warren Hollister, *The Making of England, 55 B.C. to 1399* (Lexington, Mass.: Heath, 1971), pp. 129–132.

4. Zoe Oldenbourg, *The Crusades* (New York: Pantheon, 1966), pp. 8–10.

Chapter 5. Christianity and the Early Crusades

1. Jonathan Riley-Smith, *The Crusades: A Short History* (New Haven, Conn.: Yale University Press, 1987), pp. 1–2.

2. Zoe Oldenbourg, *The Crusades* (New York: Pantheon, 1966), pp. 42–43.

3. Timothy Levi Biel, *The Crusades* (San Diego, Calif.: Lucent, 1995), p. 33.

4. Oldenbourg, pp. 48–52.

5. Riley-Smith, pp. 18–20.

6. Ibid., pp. 31–33.

7. Antony Bridge, *The Crusades* (New York: Franklin Watts, 1982), pp. 108–111.

8. Oldenbourg, pp. 149–152.

9. Riley-Smith, pp. 56–60.

10. Biel, pp. 94–95.

Chapter 6. The Second Crusade

1. Zoe Oldenbourg, *The Crusades* (New York: Pantheon, 1966), pp. 323–324.

2. William of Tyre, *Historia rerum in partibus transmarinus gestarum, XVII,* 3–6, *Patrologia Latina* 201, 675–, trans. James Brundage, *The Crusades: A Documentary History* (Milwaukee, Wis: Marquette University Press, 1962), pp. 115–121.

3. Jonathan Riley-Smith, *The Crusades: A Short History* (New Haven, Conn.: Yale University Press, 1987), pp. 102–103.

4. Timothy Levi Biel, *The Crusades* (San Diego, Calif.: Lucent, 1995), pp. 91–92.

Chapter 7. Richard I and the Third Crusade

1. Philip Henderson, *Richard Coeur de Lion: A Biography* (New York: Norton, 1959), pp. 57–59.

2. Ibid., p. 60.

3. James A. Brundage, *Richard Lion Heart* (New York: Scribner's, 1974), pp. 67–68.

4. Ibid., p. 72.

5. Ibid., pp. 80–86.

6. William Stubbs, ed., *Itinerarium Peregrinorum et Gesta Regis Ricardi,* Rolls Series (London: Longmans, 1864), vol. pp. 9–29.

7. Brundage, pp. 99–105.

Chapter 8. The Third Crusade

1. Jonathan Riley-Smith, *The Crusades: A Short History* (New Haven, Conn.: Yale University Press, 1987), pp. 111–113.

2. Zoe Oldenbourg, *The Crusades* (New York: Pantheon, 1966), pp. 449–455.

3. Ibid., p. 457.

4. Riley-Smith, p. 116.

5. Behâ-ed-Din, "Richard I Massacres Prisoners after Crusades," *Eyewitness to History,* ed., John Carey (New York: Avon Books, 1987), p. 37.

6. James A. Brundage, *Richard Lion Heart* (New York: Scribner's, 1974), pp. 125–126.

7. Ibid., pp. 144–146.

8. Ibid., pp. 146–152.

9. Riley-Smith, p. 117.

10. Oldenbourg, p. 465.

11. Bernard of Clairvaux, "In Praise of the New Knighthood," trans. Conrad Greenia Ocso, *Bernard of Clairvaux: Treatise Three, Cistercian Father Series* (Cistercian Publications, 1977) no. 19, pp. 127–145.

12. Brundage, p. 164.

13. Ibid., p. 162.

14. Ibid., pp. 162–164.

15. Ibid., pp. 165–167.

16. Caroline Bingham, *The Crowned Lions: The Early Plantagenet Kings* (Newton Abbot, England: David & Charles, 1978), p. 111.

17. Brundage, p. 167.

18. James Brundage, trans., *The Crusades: A Documentary History* (Milwaukee, Wis.: Marquette University Press, 1962), pp. 185–186.

19. Brundage, *Richard Lion Heart*, pp. 171–172.

20. Ibid., p. 173.

Chapter 9. The Trip Home

1. James A. Brundage, *Richard Lion Heart* (New York: Scribner's, 1974), pp. 174–180.

2. Graham Philips and Martin Keatman, *Robin Hood: The Man Behind the Myth* (London: Michael O'Mara, 1995), p. 2.

3. Philip Henderson, *Richard Coeur de Lion: A Biography* (New York: Norton, 1959), pp. 209–210.

4. Caroline Bingham, *The Crowned Lions: The Early Plantagenet Kings* (Newton Abbot, England: David & Charles, 1978), pp. 129–133.

5. Brundage, pp. 236–237.

6. Ibid., p. 238.

7. Ibid., p. 240.

8. Bingham, pp. 133–134.

Chapter 10. The Legacy of Richard and the Later Crusades

1. Albert Beebe White and Wallance Notestein, eds., *Source Problems in English History* (New York: Harper and Brothers, 1915).

2. Jonathan Riley-Smith, *The Crusades: A Short History* (New Haven, Conn.: Yale University Press, 1987), p. 130.

3. *Chronica Regiae Coluniensis Continuatio prima*, s.a. 1213, MGH 55 XXIV 17–18, trans., James Brundage, *The Crusades: A Documentary History* (Millwaukee, Wis.: Marquette University Press, 1962), p. 213.

4. Riley-Smith, p. 141.

5. Timothy Levi Biel, *The Crusades* (San Diego, Calif.: Lucent, 1995), p. 113.

Further Reading and Internet Addresses

Books

Child, John, Nigel Kelly, and Martyn Whittock. *The Crusades.* Lincolnwood, Ill.: NTC Contemporary Publishing, Co., 1996.

The Crusades: Failed Holy Wars. San Diego: Lucent Books, 2001.

Gibb, Christopher. *Richard the Lionheart & the Crusades.* Danbury, Conn.: Franklin Watts, 1985.

Jessop, Joanne. *Richard the Lionhearted.* New York: Bookwright, 1989.

Marshall, Chris. *Warfare in the Medieval World.* Orlando, Fla.: Raintree Steck-Vaughn Publishers, 1999.

Rice, Jr., Earle. *Life During the Crusades.* San Diego: Lucent Books, 1997.

Internet Addresses

Blanchard, Laura V. and Carolyn Schriber. "Crusades: A Guide to Online Resources." *ORB: The Online Reference Book for Medieval Studies.* 1995–1999. <http://orb.rhodes.edu/encyclop/religion/crusades/crusade.html>.

"The Crusaders." *Islam and Islamic History in Arabia and the Middle East.* n.d. <http://islam.org/mosque/ihame/Sec10.htm>.

"The Crusades." *Internet Medieval Sourcebook.* September 3, 2001. <http://www.fordham.edu/halsall/sbook1k.html>.

Dafoe, Stephen. "King Richard I – The Lionheart." *A History and Mythos of the Knights Templar—The Crusades.* 1997–2001. <http://www.templarhistory.com/richard.html>.

Dafoe, Stephen. "Saladin – Salah al-Din Yusuf bin Ayub." *A History and Mythos of the Knights Templar—The Warrior Monks.* 1997–2001. <http://www.templarhistory.com/saladin.html>.

Index